# RUSSIA

## 1941 – 1942

# BLITZKRIEG

# RUSSIA

## 1941 – 1942

### WILL FOWLER

### Ian Allan

PUBLISHING

First published 2003

ISBN 0 7110 2945 8

© Will Fowler 2003

Published by Ian Allan Publishing
an imprint of Ian Allan Publishing Ltd, Hersham, Surrey KT12 4RG.

Printed by Ian Allan Printing Ltd, Hersham, Surrey KT12 4RG.

Code: 0303/A2

Designed by Casebourne Rose Design Associates Ltd

Illustrations by Mike Rose
Maps by Sue Casebourne

Picture Credits
All photographs are from Bugle Archives.

**Cover Picture:** An infantry platoon in a typical Russian setting. The war in the East was particularly hard for the foot soldiers.

***Blitzkrieg:*** Fast armoured and mechanised warfare supported by bombers and ground attack aircraft.

# CONTENTS

## *UNTERNEHMEN BARBAROSSA*
### 6-29

The opening attacks of Operation Barbarossa seemed like a re-run of the triumph of Blitzkrieg. Tanks and vehicles plunged deep into western Russia and captured huge stocks of weapons and vast hordes of prisoners. The hope that the campaign could be concluded by the winter did not seem impossible

# THE PRICE OF VICTORY
## 30-49

A rmy Group Centre closed on Moscow, capturing huge numbers of men and equipment in pockets, or more grimly, cauldrons – Kessel. However with ruthless efficiency the Soviet government had destroyed anything they could not evacuate and moved machinery and workers to new armaments factories in the Urals.

# RASPUTITSA
## 50-69

T he onset of the autumn rains turned the dusty roads of Russia into quagmires. It became the *Rasputitsa* – the season of no roads. The German and Axis forces were now hundreds of miles from their depots at the end of appalling roads and rail links that engineers had been obliged to rebuild to European standard gauge.

# COUNTER ATTACK
## 70-94

S oviet propaganda would later portray the counter attack at Moscow as a well planned operation. It was in fact a gamble in which bitter winter weather and the exhaustion of the German forces played a very significant part along with the Soviet T-34 tank and the bravery of the Soviet soldiers.

# INDEX 95–96

# UNTERNEHMEN BARBAROSSA

*Wir rollen im wildweiten Osten*
*Auf endloser Straße dahin.*
*Wir lassen nicht rasten und rosten*
*Die Waffen, den mutigen Sinn.*
*Es dröhnen die Panzer*

*Bei Tag und bei Nacht,*
*Bis daß wir ein Ende*
*Mit Stalin gemacht.*
*Sag, Russki, ob du wohl kennst*
*Die Wagen mit dem weißen Gespenst!*

*Das Ostlandlied der Gespenster-Division*
*– The Russia Song of the Ghost Division –*

The roar of low flying aircraft, the howl of dive bombers and the crash and the sickening concussion of exploding bombs and shells that ripped apart the dawn at 03.15 on June 22, 1941 at the opening of the German offensive against the USSR literally caught the Russians napping.

The Soviet border guards were captured semi clothed as they stumbled half-awake out of their barracks. The German Army *Propagandakompanien* (PK) photographers caught the dazed look on their shocked faces as they stood with hands raised in the watery spring dawn.

## Rußlandlied

Von Alfred Heinz Jlling

Auf, Kamerad! Die Zeit ist reif —
Am Himmel steht ein Feuerschweif!
Laßt uns nicht länger warten.
Wir werfen die Propeller an!
Die Infant'rie ruft: „Marsch voran!" —
Laßt uns nach Rußland starten!
  Der Führer ruft — drum, Schatz, ade!
  Zum Siege stürmt die Ost-Armee!
  Und schlägt das dreiste Russenpack,
  Wie sie geschlagen den Polack.
  Drum, Schatz, ade, drum, Schatz, ade!
  Zum Siege stürmt die Ost-Armee!

Das Heer der Feinde schreckt uns nicht;
Wir tuen eisern unsre Pflicht
Und werden nicht verzagen, —
Bevor der Feind am Boden liegt,
Von uns vernichtet und besiegt, —
Und wir den Lorbeer tragen!
  Der Führer ruft . . . usw.

Trifft mich die Kugel gar zu gut,
So lieg ich denn in meinem Blut
In Rußlands roter Erde. —
Doch weiter stürmt das graue Heer
Und treibt den Kosak vor sich her,
Gleichwohl, ob er sich wehrte!
  Der Führer ruft . . . usw.

They were the victims of Stalin's wilful determination not to believe the evidence of his intelligence services and the warnings from Britain that an attack was impending. Prime Minister Winston Churchill contacted Sir Stafford Cripps, the British Ambassador in Moscow, in mid April with a message for Stalin:

"Following from me to M. Stalin, provided it can be personally delivered by you:

"I have sure information from a trusted agent that when the Germans thought they

**LEFT:** A postcard with the words of the *Russlandlied* – the Russia Song, optimistic propaganda at the outset of Barbarossa.

**TOP:** On the morning of June 22, 1941 German troops cross a damaged bridge over the River Bug.

**ABOVE:** Using ditches for cover a German reconnaissance patrol advances hesitantly to a Soviet held village in the Belorussia.

## RICHARD SORGE

Richard Sorge was born in Baku in 1895, the son of a German mining engineer working for the Imperial Russian Oil Company. Intriguingly, he was also the grandson of a secretary to Karl Marx. At the age of three he returned to Germany.

During World War I he served on the Western Front and was badly wounded. From 1917 to 1918 he studied at the Universities of Berlin, Kiel and Hamburg and during this time became a Communist and an active agent for the Comintern reporting to the *Glavnoye Razvedyvatel' noye Upravleniye* – GRU or "Central Intelligence Administration".

Working for a German news service he went to China and based himself in Shanghai. He then went to Tokyo working as correspondent for the *Frankfurter Zeitung*. Tall, untidy and a heavy drinker he became something of a character in the German community in Japan, particularly when he chose a flat in one of the slum districts of Tokyo. He joined the Nazi Party and this enhanced his cover. As the Press Attaché at the German Embassy in Tokyo he was a confidant of General Eugen Ott, Hitler's envoy to the Emperor.

Sorge and his Japanese assistant were finally tracked down by the Japanese counter-intelligence organisation and arrested in October 1941. It was reported that he was hanged in Tokyo on November 7, 1944.

In 1964 the USSR awarded him a posthumous "Hero of the Soviet Union" and issued a commemorative stamp showing Sorge.

**ABOVE:** Stalin's genial exterior that earned him the nickname "Uncle Joe" in Britain concealed the mind of a ruthless paranoid dictator.

had got Yugoslavia in the net – that is to say, after March 20 – they began to move three out of the five Panzer divisions from Rumania to southern Poland. The moment they heard of the Serbian revolution this movement was countermanded. Your Excellency will readily appreciate the significance of these facts."

Churchill was careful to conceal that this "sure information from a trusted agent" came from ULTRA signals intercepts. It was top grade intelligence.

In the months preceding the attack Stalin and Lavrenti Beria, his sinister chief of the NKVD secret police, had received numerous indicators that an attack was in the offing. However his deep suspicion of the West led him to believe that these might be part of a plan to entrap the USSR in a war with Germany, a country with which he had signed the Russo-German Pact on August 23, 1939.

In Germany and Western Europe the *Rote Kapelle* – Red Orchestra (the code name

**BELOW:** The thatched roof of a Soviet farm provides cover for an artillery observation post as it scans the steppe.

**ABOVE:** A machine gunner leads a patrol forward from a treeline ready to put down fire as the soldiers dash for cover.

## HITLER ON RUSSIA

❝It must never be forgotten that the present rulers of Russia are blood-stained criminals, that here we have the dregs of humanity which, favoured by the circumstances of a tragic moment, overran a great State, degraded and extirpated millions of educated people out of sheer blood-lust, and that now for nearly ten years they have ruled with such a savage tyranny as was never known before…

"It must not be forgotten that the international Jew, who is today the absolute master of Russia, does not look upon Germany as an ally but as a State condemned to the same doom as Russia."

Adolf Hitler
*Mein Kampf* – My Struggle

**ABOVE:** In the Baltic states of Latvia, Lithuania and Estonia, recently occupied by the USSR, the German forces were greeted as liberators.

**RIGHT:** One of the surviving garrison of the fortress at Brest-Litovsk emerges to surrender after putting up a heroic resistance.

given by the _Abwehr)_ – the German counter espionage organisation to the largest Soviet spy ring and resistance organisation, had been providing information to the USSR from 1938. However, in the spirit of the Russo-German Pact, Stalin had stood it down in 1939. It was reactivated following the German invasion of the USSR in 1941 and by 1942 had some 100 radio transmitters forwarding information to the USSR.

The driving force behind the _Rote Kapelle_ was Leopold Trepper, a Polish Jew who based himself in Belgium and made contact with dissident Germans. The most important of these were Harro Schulze-Boysen, grandson of Admiral von Tirpitz, and Arvid Harnack, nephew of a celebrated theologian, whose wife Mildred was American.

## *RASSENKAMPF*

Hitler characterised the war in the East as a *Rassenkampf*, a "Race War" between sub-human Slavs and superior Aryans.

In a conference with senior officers in March 1941 he said: "The war with Russia will be such that it cannot be conducted in a chivalrous fashion. This struggle is one of ideologies and racial differences and will be conducted with unprecedented merciless and unrelenting harshness."

To carry out his orders *Einsatzgruppen* (Task Forces) followed behind the armies. They were structured as *Einsatzkommandos* with a staff designated as an *Einsatzstab*. There were four groups, A, B, C and D, assigned to Army Groups North, Centre, South and the 11th Army. Their mission was to eliminate Communist officials, Jews and Roma. A specific order to murder was known as the *Kommissar Erlass*. Issued by Hitler it stated that the Soviet *politicheskii rukovoditel (politruk)*, the political officers or Commissars attached to the Red Army, "hold views directly opposite to those of National Socialism. Hence these commissars must be eliminated when captured in battle, or in resistance are on principle to be disposed of by gunshot immediately". At Kiev a total of 33,000 Jewish men, women and children were taken to the ravine at Babi Yar outside the city and machine-gunned to death by men of the *Einsatzgruppen*. In total these Task Forces killed about two million people in Poland and Russia.

**LEFT:** Fearful and hesitant, Soviet soldiers surrender to the German invaders. Regarded as subhumans many would be worked to death or murdered.

**RIGHT:** Soviet soldiers emerge from their trenches to surrender. While some groups of leaderless Russian troops put up little resistance. Others proved determined enemies who fought on even though they had been bypassed, and were waiting in ambush for German rear echelon units.

# TRADING WITH THE ENEMY

Between February 10, 1940 and June 22, 1941 the USSR had conscientiously implemented the terms of the German-Soviet agreement signed in the aftermath of the defeat of Poland. It had supplied 15,240,000kg (1,500,000 tons) of grain (rye, oats and wheat) and cotton, 101,600,000kg (1,000,000 tons) of mineral oil, 2,700kg (2.65 tons) of platinum and large quantities of strategic ores like manganese and chrome. The fuel and grain had been an important support for the Germans in their operations against the West in 1940. They were, however, slow payers and though goods worth Reich Marks (RM) 467,000,000 had been supplied to the USSR, on the day it invaded, Nazi Germany owed its enemy RM239,000,000.

To Stalin, who was always suspicious of the West, assisting Germany in the destruction of the Franco British capitalist forces may have been compensation enough.

In the Far East a brilliant but eccentric Communist agent Richard Sorge had from February 1941 been warning the Russians that the attack was in the offing.

Among the other indicators of an impending attack on the ground was the *Otto-Programme* or Otto Programme, "Otto" standing for *Ost* or East. It was the code name for the development between October 1, 1940 and May 10, 1941 of road and rail links through Eastern Europe to the borders of the USSR in preparation for *Unternehmen Barbarossa*. In 1941 the German troop strengths began to change on the Soviet German border. In early March 1941 there were 34 divisions, by April 23 this figure had risen to 59 and finally by June 5 there were 100 divisions in the East.

On June 21 a young German Communist named Korpik slipped away from his unit's concentration area in Poland and crossed the border into the USSR in order to warn them of the impending attack. Writing of the incident after the war, Nikita Kruschev, the then leader of the USSR, reported that on Stalin's orders Korpik was shot as an agent provocateur.

The German invasion plans had been

**ABOVE:** Cause – a German pioneer thrusts a demolition charge through the embrasure of a bunker on the Stalin Line.

**BELOW:** Effect – smoke rises from the smashed remains of a bunker, one of many constructed on the 1939 Soviet border.

**ABOVE:** With a PzKpfw III in the background senior officers of a Panzer Division hold a planning conference in the field.

drafted as far back as December 6, 1940 with the code name *Fall Fritz* – Plan Fritz, – however on December 18 Hitler changed the name. The huge attack would be known as *Unternehmen Barbarossa* – Operation Barbarossa – after the Emperor known as "Red Beard", the hero of the Holy Roman Empire who led the Third Crusade and died in Asia Minor. In discussion Hitler assured his generals that:

"When *Barbarossa* begins the World will hold its breath and say nothing".

**RIGHT:** The cover of *Signal,* the multilingual propaganda magazine, celebrates the unstoppable German advance into the USSR in the summer of 1941.

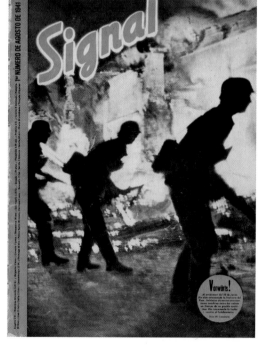

# AXIS ARMIES

### Army Group North
### *Field Marshal von Leeb*
18th Army
General George von Küchler
Pz Gruppe IV
General Erich Höppner
16th Army
General Ernst von Busch

### Army Group Centre
### *Field Marshal Fedor von Bock*
Pz Gruppe III
General Herman Hoth
9th Army
General Adolf Strauss
4th Army
General Gunther Kluge
Pz Gruppe II
General Heinz Guderian

### Army Group South
### *Field Marshal Gerd von Rundstedt*
6th Army
General Walter von Reichenau
Pz Gruppe I
General Ewald von Kleist
17th Army
General Karl Stülpnagel
Rumanian 3rd Army
General Dumitrescu
11th Army
General Eugene Schobert
Rumanian 4th Army
General Ciuperca

**ABOVE:** General Herman Hoth, Panzergruppe III.

**ABOVE:** General Ewald von Kleist, Panzergruppe I.

In a staggering example of naive wishful thinking, Stalin, who was a brutal schemer, thought the Germans would issue a formal declaration of war. The Soviet thinking was, that following a declaration of war, the size and intensity of the attack would be limited and this would allow the USSR to mobilise its reserves. There was therefore a thin skin of frontier troops but few reserves to block any German penetrations.

Work had however begun on upgrading the old pre-1939 border defences that were given the grandiloquent title of the "Stalin Line". They followed natural features like the river Velikaya to the north, the Dniepr and Pripet Marshes in the centre and the river Dniestr in the south. Though the Soviet Union never developed the sophisticated reinforced concrete defences, like the Germans with the West Wall and Atlantic Wall, they were formidable builders of well camouflaged field

**ABOVE:** German soldiers glance at Soviet prisoners being marched to the rear. The Soviet losses would seem staggering to the German troops.

**RIGHT:** The attack on the USSR would see German and Axis troops drive into a vast and inhospitable territory on a front that grew longer as they advanced eastwards. Initially it looked as if the huge gamble would pay off, but the onset of winter and increased Soviet resistance sealed the fate of this massive operation.

defences and could dig in very quickly once they had seized ground.

On June 13 the Soviet authorities in the Baltic States of Estonia, Latvia and Lithuania, sovereign countries that had been occupied by the USSR in October 1939, arrested 50,000 potential enemies who might assist the Germans.

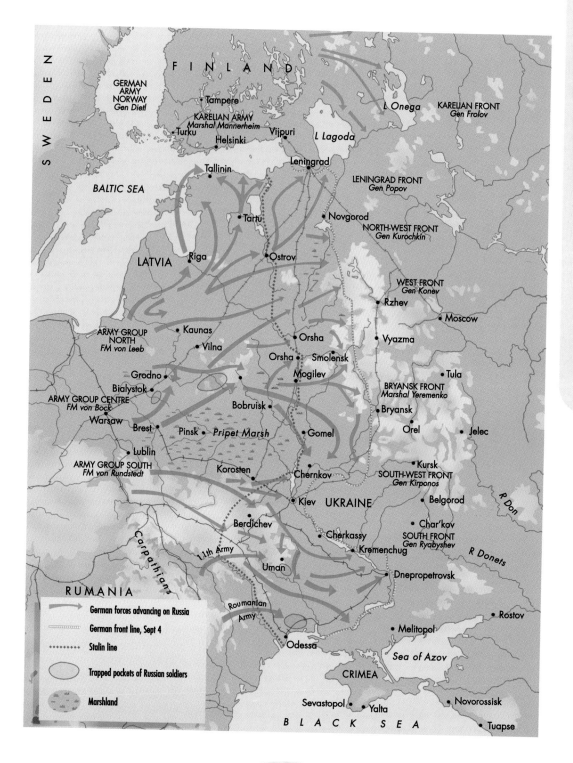

SWEDEN

FINLAND

GERMAN
ARMY
NORWAY
*Gen Dietl*

• Tampere

KARELIAN ARMY
*Marshal Mannerheim*

• Turku

Helsinki •

Vijpuri •

*L Lagoda*

*L Onega*

KARELIAN FRONT
*Gen Frolov*

BALTIC SEA

Tallinin •

Leningrad •

LENINGRAD FRONT
*Gen Popov*

Tartu •

Novgorod •

NORTH-WEST FRONT
*Gen Kurochkin*

LATVIA

Riga •

Ostrov •

WEST FRONT
*Gen Konev*

Rzhev •

• Moscow

ARMY GROUP
NORTH
*FM von Leeb*

• Kaunas

• Vilna

Orsha •

Orsha •

Smolensk •

Mogilev •

Vyazma •

• Tula

Grodno •

Bialystok •

• Tula

ARMY GROUP CENTRE
*FM von Bock*

Warsaw •

Brest •

Bobruisk •

Pinsk • *Pripet Marsh*

• Gomel

BRYANSK FRONT
*Marshal Yeremenko*

• Bryansk

Orel •

• Jelec

Lublin •

ARMY GROUP SOUTH
*FM von Rundstedt*

Korosten •

Chernkov •

• Kursk

SOUTH-WEST FRONT
*Gen Kirponos*

• Kiev UKRAINE

• Belgorod

*R Don*

Berdichev •

*11th Army*

Cherkassy •

Uman •

Kremenchug •

• Char'kov

SOUTH FRONT
*Gen Ryabyshev*

*R Donets*

Dnepropetrovsk •

*Carpathians*

RUMANIA

*Roumanian
Army*

Odessa •

• Rostov

• Melitopol

*Sea of Azov*

CRIMEA

Sevastopol •

• Yalta

• Novorossisk

• Tuapse

BLACK SEA

→ German forces advancing on Russia

·········· German front line, Sept 4

•••••••• Stalin line

⬭ Trapped pockets of Russian soldiers

Marshland

Two days later German higher formation commanders were told the date and time of the impending attack on the USSR and armoured formations began to move up under cover of the short summer night.

On June 17, Finland began a secret mobilisation. The Finns had been cultivated as potential allies by the Germans since 1940 and had agreed to seal off the northern Soviet port of Murmansk and to attack in the south east in the Lake Ladoga area near Leningrad. They were keen to reclaim the land lost to the USSR at the end of the Winter War.

On June 19 deserters from the German forces had filtered across the border and warned the Soviet forces of the impending attack. Like Korpik they were ignored, however black-outs were ordered for the major cities and towns near the border.

On the night of June 21-22 Moscow did issue orders for Western Military Districts to be brought up to combat readiness. However,

**ABOVE:** In assault order with gas masks and mess tins, German infantry move through the morning mist. Maps issued for the invasion of the USSR proved incomplete and inaccurate.

**RIGHT:** The reality of "Scorched Earth". A peasant woman watches hopelessly as her wooden home burns, torched by withdrawing Soviet troops. In the drive to deny cover and resources to their enemies both sides caused untold misery to civilians.

the orders were vague and did not call for deployment to battle positions, stating that troops were to prepare to resist "provocations" and not a full-scale attack.

On June 22 1941 at 03.15 the last illusions that an accommodation could be reached with the Nazis were shattered as German troops with their Rumanian, Finnish, and Hungarian allies punched eastwards deep into the Soviet Union. Incredibly the USSR had sent a freight train loaded with grain

# SOVIET FORCES

**Leningrad Military
District**
***General M.M. Popov***
14th Army
Lt General V.A. Frolov
7th Army
Lt General G.A. Gorelenko
23rd Army
Lt General P.S. Pshennikov

**Baltic Special Military
District**
***General F.I. Kuznetsov
(then Sobennikov)***
8th Army
Maj General P.P. Sobennikov
11th Army
Lt GeneralV.I. Morosov

**West Special Military
District**
***General D.G.Pavlov
(then Timoshenko)***
3rd Army
Lt General V.I. Kuynestov
4th Army
Maj General A.A. Korobkov
10th Army
Maj General K.D.Golubev

**Odessa Military District**
***General I.V. Tyulenev***
18th Army
Lt General A.K. Smirnov
9th Army
Lt General Ya. T.
Cherevichenko

**Kiev Special Military
District**
***General M.P.Kirponos
(then Budenny)***
5th Army
Maj General M.I. Potapov
6th Army
Lt General I.N. Muzychenko
26th Army
Lt General F. Ya Kostenko
12th Army
Maj General P.D. Ponedelin

across the bridge over the River Bug at Brest-Litovsk at 03.15 destined for Germany.

The German attack was split between three Army Groups. Army Group North under Field Marshal Ritter von Leeb consisted of 26 divisions, including three Panzer. Army Group Centre under Field Marshal Fedor von Bock consisted of 51 divisions, including nine Panzer. Finally, Army Group South under Field Marshal Gerd von Rundstedt consisted of 59 divisions, including five Panzer, 14 Rumanian and three Hungarian.

The Rumanians, like the Finns, had a grudge to settle with Stalin. The USSR had grabbed their eastern provinces of Bessarabia and Northern Bukovina in August 1939.

The German and allied forces were all supported by nine Lines of Communications Divisions. Their tasks included converting Soviet broad gauge railway track to standard European gauge and rebuilding bridges demolished by the retreating Soviet forces.

The Army Groups were backed by over 3,000 aircraft in three air fleets, *Luftflotte* I under Colonel General Alfred Keller supporting North, *Luftflotte* II under Field Marshal Albert Kesselring backing Centre and *Luftflotte* IV under Colonel General Alexander Löhr backing South. In the far north *Luftflotte* V under Colonel General Hans-Jurgen Stumpff would support the mountain troops, attack towards Murmansk. The Axis forces appeared formidable – weapons and equipment had been tested in

## MITTLERER SCHÜTZEN-PANZERWAGEN TYP HL SDKFZ 251

The design work for the superb SdKfz 251 half track that carried *Panzergrenadiere* into action began in 1935 and by the time the Ausf D model had been introduced in 1943 a total of 2,650 had been built by Borgward and Hanomag. It was a well liked and versatile vehicle, though access to the engines was difficult. The SdKfz 251 was used as the platform for support weapons as well as a command vehicle and an ambulance. It was the inspiration for the American M3 half track.

| | |
|---|---|
| Armament: | 45mm, 2 x 7.92mm MG |
| Armour: | 6mm to 13mm (0.24in to 0.51in) |
| Crew: | 3 |
| Weight: | 13,900kg (13.68 tons) |
| Hull length: | 5.66m (18ft 7in) |
| Width: | 2.29m (7ft 6in) |
| Height: | 2.42m (7ft 11in) |
| Engine: | M17-T-V-12 petrol, 500bhp |
| Road speed: | 86km/h (53.41mph) |
| Range: | 250km (155.25miles) |

battle and the men were veterans of three years of combat. They were, however, attacking an enemy of who they knew very little and across terrain that was unfamiliar. For young men who had grown up in the close country of Western Europe or the city streets of the Ruhr, Hamburg or Berlin, the

# 4.7CM PAK(T) AUF PZKPFW I

A simple but very effective modification of the PzKfwI, this self propelled anti-tank gun, the first to enter service with the German army, involved placing a Czech 4.7cm PaK M36(t) gun behind a splinter shield. The gun had a better performance than the 3.7cm on the PzKpfw III, being capable of penetrating 55mm (2.16in) at 30º at 500m (546.8yd). Between 1939 – 40 approximately 132 4.7cm PaK(t) auf PzKpfw I were built.

| | |
|---|---|
| Armament: | 4.7cm (1.85in) |
| Armour: | 10 – 13mm |
| | (0.39in – 0.51in) |
| Crew: | 3 |
| Weight: | 6,503kg (6.4 tons) |
| Hull length: | 4.42m (14ft 6in) |
| Width: | 1.85m (6ft) |
| Height: | 2.25m (7ft 4in) |
| Engine: | Maybach NL120 |
| | TKRM 100bhp |
| | petrol |
| Road speed: | 40 km/h (25mph) |
| Range: | 180km (111miles) |

| | |
|---|---|
| Armament: | 1 or 2 x 7.92mm MG |
| Armour: | 8mm to 12mm ( 0.31in |
| | to 0.47in) |
| Crew: | 2 |
| Weight: | 7,935kg (7.81 tons) |
| Hull length: | 5.8m (19ft) |
| Width: | 2.1m (6ft 10in) |
| Height: | 1.75m (5ft 9in) |
| Engine: | Maybach HL42 TUKRM |
| | 120bhp petrol |
| Road speed: | 53km/h (33mph) |
| Range: | 300km (185miles) |

# BT-7

The Soviet BT or Bystrokhodnii Tank series were Fast Tanks using the suspension developed by the irascible American inventor J. Walter Christie. The design began with the BT-2 and development went through the BT-5, climaxing with the BT-7.

Variants of the BT-7 included the BT-7A, a close support vehicle mounting the 76.2mm regimental howitzer in a larger turret with 50 rounds and two DT machine guns. It was

intended to support cavalry tank formations and carried 50 rounds of main ammunition and was slightly heavier than the BT-7.

The OP-7 was developed as a flame-thrower version which had the fuel cell for the projector in an armoured pannier on the right hull side. The BT-7 (V) or BT-7TU was the commander's model with the turret of the BT-5 (V) with radio and frame antenna, though later models had a whip antenna that made them less of an obvious target in tank-on-tank actions.

**ABOVE:** A Fieseler Fi156C *Storch* banks above a German armoured column. The versatile *Storch* was used for tasks like liaison and observation.

**LEFT:** A Swastika flag is run up the flagpole after the capture of the fortress at Brest-Litovsk.

**RIGHT:** Headed by an officer a typical German horse-drawn supply column moves along a dirt track in Russia.

open plains of the steppe and distant unattainable horizons would become oppressive. The USSR was 46 times bigger than Germany in its 1938 borders – it also had a population of 190,000,000 of whom 16,000,000 were men of military age. If it could buy time, the weight of these numbers would begin to take effect.

Though the tanks would be the cutting edge of the attacks, supported by *Panzergrenadiers* in SdKfz 251 half tracks, the bulk of German forces would advance at the same speed as Napoleon's *Grande Armée* when it entered Russia in 1812. Men marched and were backed up by horse-drawn wagons, guns and field kitchens – the German Army deployed 750,000 horses for the attack on the Soviet Union. Of the 153 divisions in *Barbarossa*,

119 still contained horse-drawn vehicles.

The Soviet forces opposite them were grouped in three groups known as Military Districts, however they had huge reserves and within six months 300 new divisions had been mobilised. The designation Military District would soon be changed to the more combative title "Front" and with it new commanders were selected not for political reliability but military competence.

On the Baltic the Soviet forces consisted of 24 divisions of which four were armoured. In the west opposite the Pripet Marshes were 30 divisions with eight armoured. Around Kiev were 58 divisions, 16 of which were armoured, while to the south on the Rumanian border were 12 divisions four of which were armoured. Though the numbers might look impressive, the divisions were not deployed to fight a defensive campaign. Many were spread to a depth of 322 to 483km (200 to 300 miles) from the border.

In the 1930s the Soviet Army had begun to upgrade its equipment and develop new tactics very similar to the "*Blitzkrieg*" of the German *Panzerwaffe* – armoured forces. However, in a frenzy of paranoia, in 1938 Stalin, convinced that political cronies and

officers were planning to overthrow him, ordered mass arrests and "Show Trials" were held in Moscow in which some 10,000 senior officers were accused of treachery. Almost all "confessed", were found guilty, and executed or sent to labour camps – *Gulag*s – in Siberia and so the Red Army lost many experienced and talented commanders, including Marshal Mikhail Tukhachevskiy, the "father" of the Soviet tank arm. It was he who laid the foundations for development work that would produce the formidable T-34 medium tank developed by the design team of M.I. Koshkin, A.A. Morozov and N.A. Kucherenko.

In the first few days of June 1941, in the air and on the ground the *Luftwaffe* destroyed 3,000 aircraft, nearly half the Red Air Force. Kesselring watched the destruction. "It seemed almost criminal to me that they should use formations which were so ridiculous from the point of view of aerial tactics, and machines obviously incapable of getting out of trouble in the air...'This is the massacre of the innocents', I thought."

The *Luftwaffe* tactical bombers attacked road and rail communications, destroyed headquarters and could even hit small targets like bunkers and trench lines. Like the campaigns in 1939 and 1940 these attacks severed the links between front line troops and their headquarters, causing a paralysis that could be exploited by mechanised forces.

In Kovel General Fedyuninsky recalled the chaos: "Railway junctions and lines of communication were being destroyed by German planes and diversionary groups. There was a shortage of wireless sets at army headquarters, nor did any of us know how to use them…Orders and instructions were slow in arriving and sometimes did not arrive at all."

By June 23 the German spearheads were 100km (62 miles) inside Russian Poland. The fortress at Brest-Litovsk on the River Bug had been by-passed and continued to hold out until July 24. The garrison was subjected to an intense bombardment including fire from the huge 60cm (23.6in) mortar, "Karl". At the close of the fighting the German 45th Infantry Division had suffered 482 killed, including 40 officers, and over 1,000 wounded – 5% of the fatal casualties suffered on the Eastern Front

in the first week of the war. Of the surviving Soviet garrison 7,000 surrendered.

Soviet armoured counter attacks north-east of Tilsit in Lithuania were beaten back with heavy losses.

On June 25 von Rundstedt's Army Group South captured Dubno and Army Group Centre manoeuvred to cut off the first pocket or *Kessel* – cauldron – of Soviet forces near Byalistok. The pocket was finally crushed on July 3, yielding 290,000 prisoners, 2,500 tanks and 1,500 guns.

With an understandable desire for vengeance Finland declared war on the USSR on June 26. A day earlier Soviet forces were reported to have attacked Finnish positions. As the men of Army Group North were welcomed as liberators in Lithuania, Army Group Centre under von Bock closed the Bialystok pocket.

The Brandenburger Special Forces went into action on June 26. A squad disguised as Soviet soldiers, commanded by Lt Wolfram

## POLIKARPOV I-153

First flown in 1938 the I-153 saw action in Finland and against the Japanese in the summer of 1939. It was outclassed by *Luftwaffe* fighters in the opening months of Barbarossa and by 1943 survivors had been relegated to second-line duties. About 20 captured aircraft were used by the Finns during the Continuation war.

| | |
|---|---|
| Type: | Single-engined fighter |
| Crew: | 1 |
| Power Plant: | One 1,000hp M-63, 9-cylinder radial |
| Performance: | Maximum speed at sea level 366km/h (227mph) |
| Maximum range: | 880km (547miles) |
| Weights: | Empty 1,452kg (3,201lb) Maximum 2,110kg (4,652lb) |
| Dimensions: | Wing span 10m (32ft 9in) Length 6.3m (20ft 8in) |
| Armament: | Four 7.62mm ShKAS MG; provision for 100kg (220lb) of bombs or six underwing 82mm RS 82 rockets. |

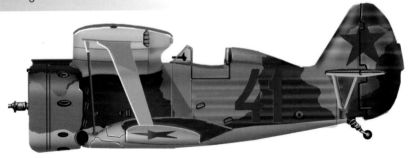

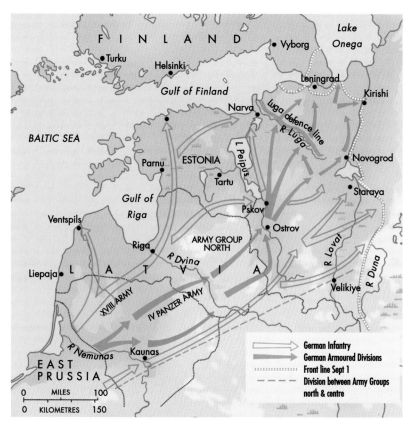

# MESSERSCHMITT BF109F-2

Almost two thirds of the *Luftwaffe* fighter squadrons that participated in the opening attacks of Barbarossa were equipped with the Bf109F. It also served with the *Afrika Korps* in North Africa. Its operational career was relatively brief being replaced by the Bf109G in 1942. The Bf109F was then passed to allied formations like the Hungarians and Croats. In the West it redressed the ascendancy gained by the RAF's new Spitfire Vs operating over northern France and the Channel.

| | |
|---|---|
| Type: | Single-engined fighter |
| Crew: | 1 |
| Power Plant: | One 1,200hp Daimler-Benz DB 601N |
| Performance: | Maximum speed at 6,000m (19,685ft) 600km/h (373mph) |
| Maximum range: | 650km (528 miles) |
| Weights: | Empty 2,353kg (5,188lb) Loaded 2,800kg (6,173lb) |
| Dimensions: | Wing span 9.9m (32ft 5in) Length 8.85m (29ft) Height 2.59m (8ft 6in) |
| Armament: | One 15mm MG 151 cannon in propeller hub, two 7.92mm (0.31in) MG 17 in upper cowling. |

Knaak, captured the strategically important bridges at Daugavpils carrying the Kovno-Leningrad highway and crossing the River Dvina. Knaak and five men were killed in the attack. One of the surviving Brandenburgers, dusty, bloodstained and exhausted, still in his Soviet uniform, was filmed by a passing PK cameraman as an example of the Soviet "subhumans" that German forces were now fighting.

Hungary declared war on the Soviet Union on June 27 and Hungarian troops came under command of von Rundstedt on July 3. The tiny Italian puppet state of Albania joined the war on the USSR on June 28.

Though the opening months of the war were a disaster for the USSR and Stalin, geography favoured the Soviet Union. Whereas in the West, Panzer Divisions were able to advance on surfaced roads and the distances

between objectives like ports, airfields and cities was comparatively short, in the USSR roads that were dirt tracks linked cities that were vast distances apart. Dust, mud and, later, extreme cold would take a toll of men and machines. Photographs showed the sweat-stained German *Landser* – "Squaddies" or "Grunts" – slogging through dust that would later turn to mud in the autumn and finally be covered in snow.

On June 29 the Finns launched an assault on the Karelian Peninsula that had been seized from them by the Soviet Union at the end of the Winter War of 1939-40. The plan envisaged a link up with Army Group North

**BELOW:** Pioneers work to rebuild a timber bridge probably burned by retreating Soviet forces. The dry riverbed will soon fill with autumn rains.

# KARL

The 60cm (23.6in) SP Mrs "Karl" were two self-propelled mortars with stumpy 5-metre (16ft 3in) long barrels christened respectively "Karl" and "Thor". They had been developed by the Germans as bombardment weapons for the French Maginot Line defences. Each had a crew of 18 and fired a 2,200kg (2.1-ton) shell. The mortars weighed 125,000kg (123 tons) and were powered by Daimler-Benz V-12 580bhp diesel engines with a top speed of 10km/h (6.2mph).
Manufactured by Rheinmetall-Borsig the overall dimensions were 11.22m (36ft 7in) long, 4.47m (14ft 6in) high, and 3.2m (10ft 5in) wide.

**ABOVE:** The 5m (16ft 3in) barrel of the 60cm mortar "Thor".

that was pushing north-eastwards through the Baltic States. Riga, the capital of Latvia, was captured on July 1 and a day later the Germans broke through the Stalin Line defences on the Latvian border.

The tanks of the II and III *Panzerarmee* encircled huge pockets of Soviet forces at Bialystock on June 30.

On July 3 Stalin broadcast to the people of the Soviet Union: "Comrades, citizens, brothers and sisters, men of the Army and Navy! I speak to you my friends.

"A grave threat hangs over our country. It can only be dispersed by the combined efforts of the military and industrial might of the nation. There is no room for the timid or the coward, for deserters or spreaders of panic, and a merciless struggle must be waged against such people."

But at this low point in the fortunes of the USSR he assured his listeners: "History shows us that there are no invincible armies."

In his broadcast Stalin ordered the implementation of a "scorched earth" policy.

"The enemy must not find a single railway-wagon, not a wagon, not a pound of bread or

**BELOW:** A former Czech Army Skoda 100mm horse-drawn field gun and limber taken into service with the German Army.

**ABOVE:** Infantry hunch around a PzKpfw III as it advances through standing crops. The PzKpfw III tank was in mass production from September 1939 to August 1943.

a glassful of petrol. All the *Kolkhozes* (collective farms) must bring in their herds and hand their stocks of wheat over to official bodies to be sent to the rear. Everything that is usable but cannot be sent back (such as wheat, petrol or non-ferrous metals) must be destroyed."

Though the British were severely stretched and the USA was not yet a belligerent in World War II, Churchill welcomed the new Communist ally in the war against Nazi Germany. On June 22 he had stated: "Any state which fights Nazism will have our aid." On the day that Stalin made his broadcast 290,000 prisoners, 2,500 tanks and 1,500 guns had been captured by the German forces who had reduced the pocket at Bialystock.

**LEFT:** With smoke from burning vehicles on the horizon, a Swastika flag is displayed as an air identification panel for *Luftwaffe* fighters and dive bombers supporting the advance.

**ABOVE:** A T-34 Ob 1940 and two T-34 Ob 1941 tanks bogged in marshland. The T-34 was a nasty shock to the Germans.

**LEFT:** A knocked out Soviet T-26S tank abandoned in a field of sunflowers.

**BELOW:** A 3.7cm Pak 35/36 crew engage light Soviet armour. The T-34 would be beyond the killing power of this anti-tank gun.

# THE PRICE OF VICTORY

*General comments: The long wait for Sondermeldung (special announcements) of new and greater victories on the Eastern Front - which have not been so late in coming in any previous campaign – is gradually causing people's expectant mood to subside.*
*Everyone in all spheres of the population is primarily concerned with rumours about the alleged very high losses among our troops.*

Sicherheitsdienst Secret Report No 208
August 4, 1941

Even though it was delivering staggering victories the German Army would not be well served by Hitler who would increasingly interfere, reduce tactical flexibility and as a result cause needless casualties. Even before the operation was launched there was a conflict of views.

The first plan drafted by General Marcks, the Chief of Staff of the 18th Army, envisaged a twin thrust at Moscow and Kiev. A huge

**ABOVE:** A trophy of war – a Soviet banner captured in the summer of 1941 is displayed for the camera.

**ABOVE:** PzKpfw III and a SdKfz 250, part of a Panzer Division, halted during one of the huge battles of encirclement.

encircling battle could be fought as the Moscow thrust swung south to link up with the Kiev axis at Kharkov. General Halder, Chief of the OKW, proposed an attack that spread the weight more equally between the north, centre and south but made Moscow the main objective. Hitler proposed that Leningrad, "the cradle of the Bolshevik revolution", should be the main objective and Moscow should be taken subsequently.

Optimistic German planners envisaged that by the onset of winter in 1941 they would be holding a line from Archangel in the north through Kotlas, Gorki, the Volga to Astrakhan in the south, designated the AA line. Optimism and ignorance also featured in the assessment of the severity of the Russian winter.

**ABOVE:** Marshal Semyon Budenny, the disastrous commander of the Soviet South West Front. Critics said his moustaches were bigger than his brains.

# T-34/76

The T34/76 had been developed from the pre-war BT series of fast tanks that used American-designed Christie suspension. The range of the T-34 could be further extended by topping up from two or four spare fuel drums carried on the rear decking.

Early T-34s had a two man hexagonal shaped all-welded turret which was cramped and lacked a radio and vision devices for the commander. The short-barrelled 7.62cm gun was soon replaced by one with a longer barrel and better anti-armour performance. It required a larger turret and this was fitted with a cupola for the commander. In June 1941 the Soviet Army had deployed 967 T-34s.

| | |
|---|---|
| Armament: | 7.62cm (3in), 2 x 7.62mm MG |
| Armour: | 18-60mm (0.71 – 2.36in) |
| Crew: | 4 |
| Weight: | 26,000kg (25.59 tons) |
| Hull length: | 5.92m (19ft 5in) |
| Width: | 3m (9ft 10in) |
| Height: | 2.44m (8ft) |
| Engine: | 500hp V-2-34 12-cylinder diesel 500hp |
| Road speed: | 54km/h (33.5mph) |
| Range: | 300km (186.3 miles) (cross country) |

## KATYUSHA

BM-13 developed in 1933 was a 16-rail 132mm (5.19in) multiple rocket launcher mounted on the 1.5-tonne GAZ-AAA truck. Soviet soldiers called it "Little Katie" or *Katyusha* after "Katerina", a popular song composed by Isakovskiy. The BM-13 could deliver a terrifying punch and the distinctive howl from the rocket motors earned it the nickname "Stalin's Organ" with German soldiers. The rails for the M13 launcher were 4,877mm (192in) long and could be elevated to 45° and traversed 10° or 20° according to the chassis. The standard Soviet MP41 mortar dial sight was used for aiming. The rockets had an 18.5kg (41lb) warhead and travelling at 355 metres (1,165ft) a second had a maximum range of 8,500 metres (5.28 miles). The 7.08kg (15.6lb)

propellant was probably solventless cordite but there are also references to Soviet munitions factories using black powder as the motor.

**ABOVE:** The 132mm *Katyusha* was mounted on US-supplied trucks after 1942.

**ABOVE:** General Heinz Guderian (right) confers with Hitler and von Bock at the Führer's HQ. As a war leader Hitler interfered and disrupted the smooth operation of Panzer formations.

By July 9 the German and Axis advance had crossed the old 1939 Russo-Polish border, swallowed up Latvia, Lithuania and most of Estonia on the Baltic, and captured Minsk, where 300,000 Soviet soldiers were trapped. On July 12 Britain and the USSR signed a mutual assistance pact and undertook not to sign a separate peace with Germany and her allies, known as the Axis.

On July 11, 1941 the tanks of General Ewald von Kleist's *Panzergruppe* I, part of Army Group South, reached the outskirts of Kiev, but bypassed the city to avoid becoming entangled in costly street fighting. The city was cut off in a huge pincer movement and after the pocket had been reduced the Germans took 665,000 prisoners, 900 tanks and 3,719 guns. The architects of this defeat were Stalin, who insisted that Kiev should be held at all costs, and his old comrade Marshal

## FIELD MARSHAL EWALD VON KLEIST

### (1881 - 1954)

Born in Brauenfels an der Lahn on August 8, 1881 von Kleist served in the General Staff in World War I. He was recalled from retirement at the outbreak of war and a *Panzergruppe* under his command achieved the decisive breakthrough in France at Abbeville in 1940. He subsequently commanded in the Balkans and Russia in 1941, and his forces captured Belgrade. He had at times an abrasive relationship with General Guderian. At the outset of Barbarossa the tanks and vehicles of their respective *Panzergruppen* I and II were painted with the letters K or G. In 1942 von Kleist commanded Army Group A that made the drive for the Caucasus oil fields in the southeast. In Russia he formed good relations with minority groups and was able to recruit Central Asian and Cossack volunteers to fight for the Germans. Captured by the British in 1945 von Kleist was transferred to the Soviet Union and died in a PoW camp at Vladimirovka near Moscow in October 1954.

Semyon Budenny. As a former NCO in the Imperial Russian Cavalry, Budenny had retained a luxuriant moustache and Russian and German senior officers were in agreement that this moustache was bigger than his brains. The implications of the moves by *Panzergruppen* I and II that would result in the huge pocket being formed to the east of Kiev were lost on him and he continued to funnel troops into a salient that would soon be cut off.

A *Kessel* was formed on July 15 as the II and III *Panzerarmee* of Army Group Centre linked up east of Smolensk. It was here in the Orsha-Smolensk area that batteries of *Katysuha* M-8 rocket launchers were deployed for the first time. Their existence had been a closely guarded secret and the crews were élite soldiers from the NKVD who were sworn to

**ABOVE:** A camouflaged SdKfz 251/3 half track heads a column of vehicles crossing a timber bridge recently constructed by German pioneers.

**ABOVE RIGHT:** Orders and maps are passed by despatch riders and *Kübelwagen* to commanders of PzKpfw IIIs, concentrated prior to an attack. German tank crews were now very experienced.

**RIGHT:** A T-34 Ob 1941 burns. Though crudely finished its tough angled armour made it vulnerable only to the battle proven 8.8cm Flak gun used in a ground role.

the destruction of the equipment if there was a risk of capture and even suicide to ensure that the enemy would not acquire the secrets of the system

The success of the German deep armoured

# BLITZKRIEG

attacks that were now universally known as *Blitzkrieg* – lightning war – was exhilarating and almost bewildering. Hitler's interference was confusing for the officers who were delivering this success.

On July 19, at the pretentiously named *Wolfsschanze* – The Wolf's Lair – Hitler's HQ in Rastenburg, East Prussia, he issued Directive No 33 in which he stated that the priorities were now to be Leningrad and the Ukraine. If the senior OKW staff questioned these changes Hitler would silence them by saying that they did not understand economics and that the coal, wheat and factories of the Don Basin and Ukraine were the target to the south. To achieve this Army Group Centre was ordered to transfer its tanks from the powerful *Panzergruppe* to the two Army Groups to the north and south. The *Luftwaffe* however was ordered to launch air

**ABOVE:** Flowers for the victors – Ukrainians greet German motorcycle reconnaissance troops.

## PULEMET DEGTYAREVA PEKHOTNII (DP)

The Soviet *Pulemet Degtyareva Pekhotnii* (DP) light machine gun was designed in the 1920s by Vasily Alexeyevich Degtyarev, an engineer at the Tula arsenal. The DP was a simple gas-operated weapon with only six moving parts. The gun had been adopted by the Soviet Army in 1928 following two years of trials. Despite these trials during the war the DP was revealed to have a return spring that weakened after sustained periods of firing and a bipod that had a tendency to buckle when the gun was placed heavily in position. It weighed 11.9kg (26.2lb) and fired from a 47-round drum magazine at 520 to 580 rounds a minute, a rate that made for accurate shooting and ammunition conservation. A DP crew carried three drum magazines in a metal box.

**ABOVE:** A PzKpfw 35(t) tank of Army Group North moves cautiously through heavily wooded terrain during the drive on Leningrad.

**BELOW:** Roughly camouflaged Red Air Force Polikarpov I-15 fighters captured by advancing German forces. Twenty-two were passed to the Finns.

**ABOVE:** *Landsers* – German infantry – march eastwards following up the Stukas and tanks of the *Blitzkrieg*.

**LEFT:** With its rear deck cluttered with spare kit and track links a PzKpfw III grinds through Belorussia.

**TOP RIGHT:** A *Lotta* (Finnish Army Nurse) feeds a wounded Finnish soldier during fighting near Leningrad.

**RIGHT:** A Finnish soldier armed with a Konepistool m/31 submachine gun shelters in a waterlogged communication trench.

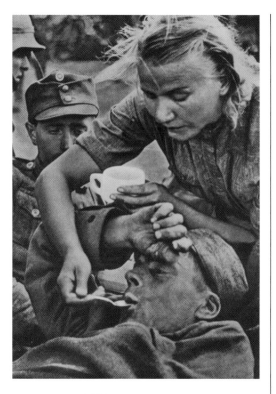

## DIVISION AZUL

The *Division Azul* – Blue Division – or 250th Division initially commanded by Major General Augustin Muñoz Grandes was composed of Spanish volunteers and derived its nickname from the blue Falangist shirts worn by many of its members. General Francisco Franco, the Fascist *Caudillo* (Leader of Spain), kept the country neutral, but allowed Spaniards to volunteer for service against the USSR. It is estimated that 47,000 Spaniards served in the division between 1941 and 1944 and though officially it had been disbanded in 1943 these men became part of a smaller Spanish Legion. In August 1942 the division, composed of the 262nd, 263rd and 269th Regiments, was assigned to the 54th Corps near Leningrad and in fighting in February 1943 suffered 2,253 casualties near Krasny Bor. Muñoz Grandes was succeeded by Major General Esteban Infantes in December 1942. In total the Division suffered 22,000 casualties, 4,500 were killed or died and fewer than 300 prisoners of war returned from the USSR in 1954.

attacks on Moscow. In the first, by Kesselring's *Luftflotte* II on July 22, 127 aircraft hit the Soviet capital. During the rest of the year there were 75 attacks, but 59 were by formations of 59 aircraft or less.

Tallinin, the capital of the northern Baltic state of Estonia, fell to Army Group North on July 27 and the Germans pushed remorselessly towards the city of Peter the Great, that had been renamed Leningrad after Lenin's death. The city had been the centre of the 1905 Russian Revolution and in the Bolshevik

## STARVATION

The lack of preparation by the political bosses and military commanders in Leningrad became evident when on September 1, 1941, rations for manual and office workers were set at respectively 600 and 400 grams (21oz and 14oz) of bread a day, with 300 grams (10.5oz) for dependants. In an air raid on the night of September 8 the Badaev food warehouse was hit by incendiaries and burned down. Two days later rations were reduced for manual workers to 500 grams (17.6oz), for office workers to 300 grams and children

and dependants to 250 grams (8.8oz) a day. A day later electricity was rationed to a few hours a day. By November the workers were receiving 250 grams and the bread itself was made from 2% flour, 3% corn flour and 73% rye flour, the rest being bulked out with ingredients used in industrial processes like linseed oil cake and cellulose.

**BELOW:** A body is delivered to a crude graveyard in Leningrad with the dead wrapped in blankets on the surface. In the background are tethered barrage balloons.

Revolution, civil war and collapse of the administration in 1917, starvation and near siege conditions had reduced the population from 2,100,000 in 1914 to 770,000 by 1920. Now it was to undergo a harsher punishment.

Leningrad would be besieged by Army Group North for 900 days. By the time it was finally liberated in January 1944 over 600,000 Leningraders had starved to death and 200,000 had been killed by the German bombardment. As starvation set in with the onset of winter those who could find a few frozen potatoes, some glue or linseed oil, or a share in a dead horse, dog or rat regarded themselves as lucky.

**BELOW:** Soviet anti-aircraft crews man a sound detector and await approaching German bombers. The *Luftwaffe* attacks on Moscow were never as heavy as those on London a year earlier.

**ABOVE:** A park of knocked out Soviet T-26 light tanks. Armed with a 45mm gun and with a crew of three the T-26s had seen action in Finland, but were no match for the German panzers.

Army Group North reached Lake Ilmen and the ancient city of Novgorod on July 31. The advance was slowing down, partly because of the limited routes through areas of dense woodland, but also because the soldiers – particularly the infantry – were exhausted. Later in the year at Novgorod they would be joined by a new allied formation, Spanish volunteers whose unit was nicknamed the Blue Division.

On August 5 the Smolensk pocket surrendered and 310,000 Soviet prisoners were captured. Two days later to the south the reduction of the Uman pocket containing the Soviet 6th, 12th and 18th Armies was announced and with it the capture of 100,000 prisoners, 317 tanks and 858 guns.

On August 7 the men of the *Corpo di spedizione italiano in Russia* (CSIR), three Italian

**ABOVE:** Knocked out BT-7 fast tanks abandoned on the road to Leningrad. The BT-7 used the sophisticated American Christie suspension.

**BELOW:** Soviet 7.62mm water-cooled Maxim machine guns and 37mm AA guns in an anti-aircraft battery captured intact by advancing German ground troops.

**ABOVE:** A farmyard serves as a temporary holding area for Soviet PoWs in the autumn of 1941. The Russian losses in men and equipment appeared fatal to OKW staff.

**BELOW:** Abandoned Soviet helmets. The design was based on a modified version of the Swiss Army helmet and would remain in use in Russia into the 21st century.

infantry divisions, *"Pasubio"*, *"Torino"* and *"Celere"*, went into action in Russia. Under General Giovanni Messe they formed part of the German 11th Army. Hitler had kept *Barbarossa* a secret from Mussolini until the day of the attack, but the *Duce* had demanded that the dignity of Fascist Italy would not allow her to shirk her part in the "Crusade against Bolshevism".

By August 13, the 53rd day of the war in the East, German casualties had reached a total of 389,924 of whom 98,600 were killed or missing. These figures were a grim contrast with the 218,109 casualties and 97,000 dead of the years September 1939 to May 1941 that encompassed the campaigns in Poland, Norway, France, the Balkans and North Africa. They were a portent of what was to come.

**ABOVE:** Hitler and Mussolini photographed by a *Luftwaffe* cameraman emerge from a Ju52 during a visit in the summer of 1941 by the two leaders to the Eastern Front.

**TOP RIGHT:** Italian cavalry leave their mounts in the cover of an anti-tank ditch as they move forward to scout a Soviet position.

**RIGHT:** An Italian flame thrower crew in action. Italian troops were employed in the siege of Odessa on the Black Sea.

On the coast of the Black Sea the Rumanian Army cut off the port of Odessa and established a siege. In the last two months of October 1941 Major General I.Y. Petrov led 32,000 troops, the survivors of the Independent Maritime Army, from Odessa to

**ABOVE**: *Landsers* and a horse-drawn supply column slog past one of the numerous military cemeteries that were appearing in Russia and the Ukraine.

**RIGHT:** The smashed and smoking wreckage of a convoy of Soviet ZIS-32 4x4 3-ton trucks hit by *Luftwaffe* ground-attack aircraft.

Sevastopol aboard 37 large transports and numerous smaller vessels. The evacuation largely carried out on the night of October 15/16 was an operation as impressive as that by the Royal Navy at Dunkirk a little over a year earlier. The decision to abandon Odessa made sound military sense since if Sevastopol fell Odessa was doomed.

By September 4 the Finns had closed up to their original border with the USSR but were unwilling to move closer than 40km (25 miles) to Leningrad for political reasons.

**ABOVE:** Men of the *Waffen-SS* cavalry rest during the summer battles in 1941. Cavalry was used for scouting and reconnaissance operations.

**BELOW:** A BA-10 armoured car and truck among the animal and human victims of the rapidly advancing German army in Russia.

**LEFT:** Red Navy gunners with a triple 7.62mm Pulemet Maksima Obrazets 1910 Maxim anti-aircraft machine gun, a configuration that was capable of 2,080 to 2,400 rounds a minute.

Their leader Marshal Baron Gustav von Mannerheim had come into the war to recover the territory lost in the Winter War. To the south Army Group North closed up to the city and when on June 22 the IV *Panzerarmee* reached the old fortress of Shlisselburg on Lake Ladoga to the east, Leningrad was cut off from land links. If the Finns had been committed to attacking the city Field Marshal von Leeb was convinced that in the late summer of 1941 the German and Finnish troops could have jointly captured it.

On September 5 Hitler changed his mind again. Moscow would now be the priority. Army Groups North and South were ordered to hand over or return the armoured forces that had been loaned to them or were under command. In the south this was easier to order than implement: Army Group South had surrounded the huge pocket at Kiev and was in the process of reducing it. It was a major victory but would delay the drive on Moscow and so give the Soviet Army and civilians enough time to construct defences around the city. The work was largely undertaken by women who in November built 1,428 artillery and machine gun positions, dug 160km (100 miles) of anti-tank ditches and laid 112km (70 miles) of triple coil barbed wire obstacles as part of the city's outer defences.

Hitler never fully grasped the scale of operations in Russia. The victories in Poland and

**LEFT:** A sniper with a 7.62mm Samozariadnyia Vintovka Tokareva o1940g or SVT40 automatic rifle. The SVT40 had a heavy recoil, ten-round box magazine and weighed 3.89kg.

**ABOVE:** Field Marshal Ritter von Leeb who commanded Army Group North until he was relieved by Hitler on January 16, 1942.

the West had been because roads were good or the distances short. The Germans were attacking from well-stocked and accessible depots and the action was so fast that Hitler had little chance to interfere. Had he made Moscow the priority target from the outset the two *Panzergruppen* that straddled the Moscow highway, the only metalled road outside of the cities, could have used it to push through to the city. If Moscow had been captured, it might have been fought for like Stalingrad a year later, but capturing it would have been a savage blow to Russian morale. It would also have severed the north-south rail communications in the USSR. Stalin might have taken the USSR out of the war even before the USA had joined the fight against Nazi Germany.

# RASPUTITSA

*"We have seriously underestimated the Russians, the extent of the country and the treachery of the climate. This is the revenge of reality".*

*Colonel General Heinz Guderian*
*Letter to his wife November 9, 1941*

On September 27 the first autumn rains began to fall, they would create the *rasputitsa* – "the season of no roads" – in which dusty tracks became deep muddy sloughs that halted or slowed down men and vehicles. The *rasputitsa* occurred twice a year, in the autumn rains and in the spring thaw. Known by the Germans as the *Schlammperiode* it had a significant effect on operations between 1941 and 1944 and could stop or slow down Soviet as well as German offensives.

Three days after the first rain, Operation *Taifun* (Typhoon) was launched with Moscow as its objective. The II *Panzerarmee* and *Panzergruppen* III and IV faced three Soviet Fronts: the West Front under General Ivan Konev composed of seven armies, the Bryansk Front under General Andrey Eremenko with three armies, and in the rear

Stalin's old comrade from the Civil War, the incompetent Marshal Semyon Budenny, commanded the Reserve Front of five armies.

It was a formidable force but a greater threat was "General Winter", the severe Russian winter that was beginning to show itself following the autumn rains. The poor roads caused the German supply system to break down and the delivery of food, fuel and ammunition became erratic.

At Bryansk the II *Panzerarmee* under Guderian quickly cut off and surrounded Soviet forces in a pocket, while to the north the 9th Army under General Strauss and the

**LEFT:** The crew of a BMW R75 from a motorised infantry regiment struggle through the rutted dust of a Russian road. Dust would clog engines and cause excess wear.

**ABOVE:** A *Waffen-SS* 4 x 2 Kfz 15, formerly a British Army Morris-Commercial 8-cwt truck captured in 1940, churns through the mud.

**RIGHT:** A motorcycle completely clogged with mud. The soft mud offered no traction as well as seeming to be almost bottomless.

4th Army under Field Marshal von Kluge cut off another group at the railway town of Vyazma. Bryansk and the bridge over the Desna had been taken in a swift coup on October 6 by the men of General von Arnim's

17th Panzer Division. It was full of troops, heavy artillery and NKVD units and in store for a planned defence were 100,000 Molotov cocktails – petrol bombs. Its capture put one of the most important railway junctions in European Russia in German hands.

The German forces were closing in on Moscow and still inflicting staggering defeats on the Soviet Army. In Berlin on October 3 Hitler boasted:

"Russia has already been broken and will never rise again".

On October 10, General Zhukov took over command of the West Front and with it the defence of Moscow. The Front consisted of eight armies on a 280km (174-mile) line centred on Mozhaisk 100km (62 miles) west of Moscow. Four days later the Bryansk pocket surrendered and though many men

had been able to break out eastwards some 50,000 began the grim march westwards to camps in Poland.

Like a military dilettante Hitler now changed his mind again – Moscow was not to be attacked directly, it was to be outflanked.

Fear gripped the city in mid October. Though Stalin remained in the capital most of the foreign embassies and the government ministries were evacuated to Kuibyshev behind the River Volga. The British and American Defence attaches were convinced that the capital would fall. Martial law was declared and even the jails were scoured for likely reinforcements. An office in the Kremlin with a window visible to Muscovites in Red Square was reported to be Stalin's and at night the light was left on to convince the citizens that he was at work.

Significantly early in the war the Soviet Union had already started dismantling its major armaments factories and moving them by rail hundreds of kilometres to the east

## DOG MINES

In late October the 1st, 3rd and 7th Panzer Divisions encountered a startling new Soviet anti-tank weapon – the dog mine. The dogs, that became known to the Germans as *Hundminen*, carrying high explosives in two canvas bags, or an anti-tank mine strapped to their back, had been trained to run under enemy tanks. The charge in its harness was linked to a hinged wooden lever that detonated it when it was depressed. The dog mines were deployed by the 2nd Army Destroyer Detachment based at Vishnyaki near Moscow. There were about 235 armed dog handlers to a detachment. The detachments made up a "destroyer battalion" of 500 men. The dogs, that were from a number of breeds including Dobermans and Alsatians, had been trained to run under tractors with their engines running in order to retrieve food. Since the belly armour of a tank is the weakest part, a charge exploding beneath it could cripple or destroy the tank. German soldiers, consequently, shot any dogs that they encountered in the front line.

**TOP LEFT:** The pioneer helmsmen on a *Sturmboot* assault boat transports an infantry section across a Russian river. Some of these rivers were vast. Navigable waterways were a major obstacles, however the speed of the German advance meant that Soviet forces were unable to form a defence.

**LEFT:** One of the members of an MG34 crew in the assault boat. He has the metal spare barrel container slung over his shoulder. The high rate of fire of the machine gun obliged the crew to change barrels after firing 500 rounds to prevent overheating.

**ABOVE:** An MG34 in action – a versatile pre-war design that was the world's first General Purpose Machine Gun (GPMG).

beyond the Ural Mountains. Though this had caused considerable disruption it now placed them out of range of the *Luftwaffe*. At Chelyabinsk the production lines of the huge Tankograd tank factory were producing the T-34. Conditions in these factories were as grim as anything in the front line with workers putting in long hours on minimal rations. Berte Mendeleeva recalled of Tankograd:

"The machinists in the workshops were mainly women and even teenagers. Some were so young that they needed to stand on boxes to reach the work bench." They worked in appalling conditions. At one tank factory, in the evening 8,000 female workers

The USSR mobilised women to work in factories and even in the front line as tank crews. It was the only country to send them into action in the air.

When in October 1941 Marina Raskova, a vivacious 28-year-old pilot and navigator, who had won the Gold Star of the Soviet Union for her pioneering work in 1938, proposed that women should fly and service combat aircraft, large numbers of women came to Moscow.

About 1,000 were selected, among them Lilya Litvak who joined the 586th Fighter Regiment. Twice wounded in action, Litvak, flying the Yak-1, became the highest scoring female fighter pilot with 12 kills and three shared victories, before she was killed in action in August 1943.

Marina Raskova was promoted to Major and since she was more skilled as a navigator than a pilot, elected to lead the 587th Dive Bomber Regiment which was later given the honorific title of the 125th M.M. Raskova Borisov Guards Bomber Regiment. She flew the twin-engined Pe-2 dive bomber but tragically was killed in 1943 before she could lead the regiment in action.

The first all-female formation to be activated was the 588th Air Regiment that went into action in the summer of 1942. By October 1943 its performance had earned it the title 46th Taman Guards Bomber Regiment. The women flew the fragile Po-2 biplane. It was terribly vulnerable and so attacks were conducted at night from altitudes of between 600 and 1,200 metres (2,000 to 4,000ft).

For the Germans the Po-2's 100hp radial engine sounded like a malign sewing machine and when they discovered that some

# THE NIGHT WITCHES

of these front line intruders were piloted by women the pilots of the 46th Guards Regiment earned a new title for the Germans, they were "The Night Witches".

The 46th was the only all-women regiment in the Red Army with a total strength of over 200. It was commanded by Major Yevdokiya Bershanskaya throughout the war. The 46th was composed of three squadrons with a training squadron. Thirty air crew were killed during the war and the regiment flew over 24,000 combat missions in 1,100 nights. It was the most decorated of the women's formations with 23 members receiving the Gold Star of the Hero of the Soviet Union, the nation's highest award – five posthumously. The

Regiment adopted the slogan: "You are a woman, and you should be proud of that".

The second commander of the 125th Bomber Regiment after Marina Raskova's death was a man, Lt Col Valentin Markov. When the war ended he married a navigator from the regiment. During the war fifteen women were killed in action and five became Heroes of the Soviet Union.

Women also flew with male formations. One of them, Senior Lieutenant Anna Timofeya-Yegorova, was the deputy commander of the 805th Ground Attack Regiment flying the heavily armoured Illyushin Shtumovik.

## POLIKARPOV U-2VS (PO-2)

First flown in January 1928, over 13,000 had been built by June 1941. Though it was used primarily for training and liaison, it pioneered night raids. A number of captured aircraft were flown by ex-Soviet Air Force volunteer personnel for the *Luftwaffe* in night attacks in the Eastern Front. Production continued into the mid 1950s in eastern Europe.

| | |
|---|---|
| Type: | Close-support light bomber |
| Crew: | 2–3 |
| Power Plant: | One 100hp M-11 |
| Performance: | Maximum speed at sea level 150km/h (93mph) |
| Maximum range: | 530km (239miles) |
| Weights: | Empty 635kg (1,400lb) Loaded 890kg (1,962lb) |
| Dimensions: | Wing span upper 11.4m (37ft 5in) Wing span lower 10.65m (34ft 11in) |
| Length: | 8.15m (26ft 9in) |
| Armament: | One 7.62mm ShKAS MG in rear cockpit; max bomb load 250kg (550lb) or rocket projectiles under wing. |

were housed in timber and earth bunkers.

The weapons and vehicles they produced were by Western standards crudely finished, but they worked and were becoming available in quantity. Tanks were also being built closer to the front at Gorki and Kirov – the USSR was already beginning to win the production battle.

On October 18 men of the German 9th Army reached Mozhaisk and penetrated the outer defence line of Moscow. They were now only 160km (100miles) from the capital. A day later the Vyazma pocket collapsed yielding some 670,000 prisoners from 67 Infantry Divisions, six Cavalry Divisions and various armoured formations and with them 1,000 tanks and 4,000 guns.

On October 30 the II *Panzerarmee* failed to

**ABOVE:** A column of supply wagons moves along a muddy, but viable, road. In later years Partisan attacks would make these "safe" areas behind the lines another war zone.

**ABOVE RIGHT:** PzKpfw IV Ausf F tanks at dawn. They were armed with the short-barrelled 7.5cm gun and were outclassed by the Soviet T-34/75, and particularly the T-34/85.

**RIGHT:** German walking wounded make their way to the rear. The Eastern Front would prove staggeringly costly in men and equipment.

capture Orel because it was almost out of fuel and the mud had reduced the mobility of those tanks still full of fuel. There was a pause as reinforcements and supplies were moved

## BOLT ACTION

The *Karabiner* 98 *kurz* – Kar 98k or Short '98 Carbine – the bolt action rifle that armed the bulk of German soldiers in the East, was developed from the Mauser commercial rifle called the Standard Model, first produced in 1924 in Belgium. The Kar 98k produced in 1935 weighed 3.9kg (8.6lb), was 1,107.5mm (43.6 in) long, and in its ten-year production life it was also manufactured in thousands in Germany, by FN in Belgium and Brno in Czechoslovakia.

A trained soldier armed with a Kar 98k could fire at 15 rounds a minute, however, like the Gewehr 98, the new rifle had only a five-round magazine, which could be a liability in a fire fight. Like all the 7.92mm calibre rifles, the maximum effective range of the Kar 98k was 800 metres (2,624.6ft).

**ABOVE:** A 57mm Model 1941 anti-tank gun captured by a German PzKpfw III. It would later be used against Soviet and Allied tanks.

**BELOW:** An Italian anti-tank gun crew in action. Blankets appear to have been draped over the shield to enhance camouflage.

up for the attack on Moscow.

On November 7 snow and frost had frozen the soft mud so that vehicles could move more freely and the decision was taken to attack again. By now an estimated 80 Soviet divisions were in position in front of Moscow. In just over two weeks of hard fighting the Germans pushed to positions 60km (37 miles) north west of Moscow. Reconnaissance patrols from the 2nd Panzer Division under Lt General Decker reached Ozeretskoye and were able to pick up discarded tram tickets, with word *MOCKBA*, at the terminus stop. In the south troops reached Kashira on the River Ugra 120km (74 miles) from Moscow.

In his order of the day to the *Panzergruppe* IV on November 17 General Erich Höpner wrote:

**ABOVE:** A well spaced Axis convoy in the spring snow. Large gaps between the vehicles would make them less vulnerable to air attack. In the foreground is an Italian Fiat 628BL Mil 4 x 2 Medium Cargo Truck.

## FEAR IN MOSCOW

The national Defence Committee appeals to all the workers of Moscow to observe order, remain calm and give their entire support to the Red Army in defence of the capital.

Moscow National Defence Committee October 20, 1941

**ABOVE:** Assault troops storm into the smoking remains of a Soviet bunker. Demolition charges, flame throwers and point-blank artillery or tank gunfire would be used to destroy bunkers.

"Arouse your troops into a state of awareness. Revive their spirit. Show them the objective that will mean for them the glorious conclusion of a hard campaign and the prospect of well-earned rest. Lead them with vigour and confidence in victory!

"May the Lord of Hosts grant you success!"

By December 1941 the German forces had taken 3,350,639 prisoners, aside from the huge casualties they had inflicted on the Soviet Army. The pages of newspapers in Germany were filled with pictures of burning or wrecked vehicles and columns of tired, scruffy, starving prisoners plodding westwards.

Now all that remained for the German forces was a final push to capture Moscow and, in Hitler's words at the beginning of *Barbarossa*, to watch as "the whole rotten structure (comes) crashing down". The thrust that finally came to an exhausted halt

**ABOVE:** Desperate Soviet PoWs struggle to lap up water from a semi-frozen stream. The brutal neglect of their captives by the Germans forced many Soviet soldiers into similar humiliating scenes.

on December 5, when Hitler ordered that the winter operations should stop, was in places actually to the east of Moscow.

Moscow is on the 37th Meridian. When the 29th Motorised Infantry Division, part of General Guderian's II *Panzerarmee*, reached Mikhaylov they were actually on the 39th Meridian, about 150km (93 miles) south and 30km (18½ miles) east of the Soviet capital.

The defences at the city of Tula on the River Don, known as "little Moscow", which were

**RIGHT:** Huddled in tattered greatcoats Soviet prisoners glance up at the *Signal* photographer as they are marched westwards in the winter of 1941. Images like this were paraded in Germany to show that the Russians were "subhuman".

commanded by General Katukov, held on and this prevented the tanks from rolling up the front. To the north of the city the tanks of General Erich Höppner's *Panzergruppe* IV had reached the Volga canal at Yakhroma and at Krasnaya Polyana, the outer suburbs of Moscow. Here they were halted by the defences manned by the 20th and 33rd Armies of the Soviet Western Front.

The 7th Panzer Division – Rommel's old *Gespenster-Division* (Ghost Division), now part of *Panzergruppe* III commanded by General Reinhardt – reached the Moscow-Volga canal to the north of the city and actually crossed it at Dmitrov but was thrown back by a vigorous Soviet counter-attack.

In his headquarters in a farmhouse near Tolstoy's *dacha* at Yasnaya Polyana, Guderian wrote bitterly to his wife:

"The icy cold, the wretched accommodation, the insufficient clothing, the heavy losses of men and matériel, and the meagre supplies of fuel are making military opera-

tions a torture, and I am getting increasingly depressed by the enormous weight of responsibility which, in spite of all fine words, no-one can take off my shoulders."

On December 8, as winter gripped Russia, the German commanders realised that they must dig in to see out one of the coldest winters on record. The thermometers now registered -35°C (-31°F). The German armies had suffered 250,000 dead and twice that number of wounded and by the end of the year were 340,000 under strength. Troop reinforcements were being transferred from France to bring formations up to strength. A soldier in the 69th Rifle Regiment in the 10th Panzer Division confided ruefully to his diary: "We are waging the winter war as if this was one of our Black Forest winters back home." Of the 26 supply trains required daily by Army Group Centre only eight or ten were making it through the bitter weather.

Life might be grim for the ill-equipped German and Axis soldiers but across the

**FAR LEFT:** A knocked out PzKpfw IV with its turret traversed left and engine louvres open. It has been caught in a built up area – the most vulnerable location for armoured vehicles.

**LEFT:** A weary MG34 gunner in a blazing town. Buildings were torched by both sides in an attempt to deny cover as the winter approached – the chief sufferers were the civilians.

front lines A.M. Samsonov, the Soviet official historian, described the fear that gripped Moscow:

"A mood of alarm spread in the city. The evacuation of industrial undertakings, Ministries, authorities, and institutions was speeded up. There were also, at that time, sporadic cases of confusion among the public. There were people who spread panic, who left their place of work and hastened to get out of the city. There were also traitors who exploited the situation in order to steal socialist property and who tried to undermine the power of the Soviet State."

Richard Sorge's warnings about *Barbarossa* may have been ignored but his most important information for Stalin was that the Japanese did not intend to capitalise on the Soviet Union's misfortunes in 1941 and invade from Manchuria. The Japanese *Kwantung* Army in Manchuria was an élite force and consequently the Soviet forces deployed opposite it were of an equally high standard. Sorge's intelligence allowed the *Stavka* (Soviet High Command) to move these last available reserves, eight tank brigades and 34 high-quality Siberian divisions, from the east and employ them in the counter attack at Moscow in the winter of 1941-1942.

In Germany the gravity of the threat in the East became evident on December 20, when Joseph Goebbels launched an appeal for winter clothing for troops in the East. It would yield a curious mixture of winter sports clothing and high-fashion garments like fur coats and hats. In the east Soviet soldiers were capturing Germans who were wearing their drill fatigue uniforms over their worn serge tunics and trousers and bulking them out with waste paper, including surrender leaflets that had not been dropped over Soviet lines. Whitewash was painted onto tanks and vehicles and bed sheets used as improvised personal camouflage.

Experienced German soldiers from the eastern territories of the Third Reich knew that winters could be severe and would wear slightly larger jackboots that could be padded out with insulation. However men wearing steel helmets and steel-studded boots conducted cold through their heads and feet.

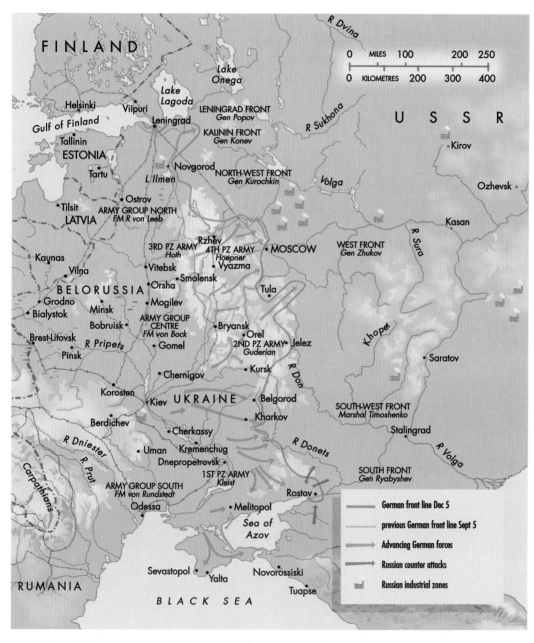

**LEFT:** Junkers Ju52 transports would be a vital link to forward troops, supplying desperately needed supplies to the many isolated small pockets that were cut off from the main force in the winter of 1941-42.

**ABOVE:** The German penetration into Russia and the Ukraine took them east of Moscow. The fierce Russian winter and almost total exhaustion of the men meant that the German forces were incapable of taking the capital.

The cold was so severe that the *ersatz* rubber of wheels and tyres, named after the Buna factory where it was developed, turned to the consistency of wood and mineral oils became thick and ceased to lubricate weapons. Unprotected hands froze to exposed metal parts of weapons and vehicles and frostbite became as great a danger as the marauding Soviet forces. General Schaal reported to Guderian that tank engines had to be warmed up for 12 hours before they would move. The horses that had accompanied the German forces from Europe suffered cruelly in the Russian winter. Oats and fodder were in short supply and unlike tough Russian ponies they could not use their hoofs to clear the snow and graze on winter grass. German soldiers took the caps, gloves, boots and quilted coats from the Soviet dead and when they robbed prisoners of their clothing effectively condemned them to death in the extreme cold.

**ABOVE:** A sentry on guard in the snow gives little indication of how bitterly cold it would become in Russia on this front cover of *Die Wehrmacht*.

**LEFT:** Bicycle-riding infantry in the early winter look almost like uniformed tourists against the background of a Russian Orthodox monastery.

In contrast to the Germans, Soviet troops were excellently equipped. Beneath their white camouflaged smocks and trousers the men wore a padded *telogreika* or sheepskin jacket, padded trousers (*vatnie sharovari*), a *shapka-ushanka* fleece cap and sometimes *valenki* compressed felt boots, a superior and much prized version of which had a waterproof rubber sole. In Moscow in the winter of 1941 the clothing factories had produced 326,700 pairs of *valenki* and 264,400 fur gloves.

Soviet cavalry and ski troops were also able to move freely across the snow and frozen rivers outflanking German positions. As their resources had been stretched the German armies had relied on mobile patrols

**ABOVE:** An MG34 crew with the gun on its sustained-fire tripod dash forward in the snow. Many men were not as lucky as this crew and lacked even greatcoats.

and artillery fire to cover the gaps between their positions and it was through these gaps that Soviet troops were able to filter. Not all the Soviet soldiers who went into action in the winter of 1941 were tough and experienced, many were under or over age and had had limited training, however there enough troops from the Siberian armies to give them backbone.

The first indication to German forces that new forces might be being deployed around Moscow came in early December from the

**LEFT:** The killing pace takes its toll on an exhausted German despatch rider.

**BELOW:** The crew struggle to free their BMW R71 from the Russian mud.

electronic warfare detachment of the 45th Infantry Division's 135th Infantry Regiment in the village of Yelets on the right flank of the German advance. Hooking into a Soviet telephone landline they picked up references to "*the Khabarovsk lot*". Khabarovsk was the city where the Far Eastern Army "Special Corps" had been established by Marshal Tukhachevskiy in the early 1930s. It was a force that by 1936 consisted of 60,000 serving soldiers and 50,000 reservists who were now peasant farmers. Tukhachevskiy had established this military community as a barrier against Japanese attacks from Manchuria.

**ABOVE:** An infantry platoon in a typical Russian setting. The war in the East was particularly hard for the foot soldiers.

**ABOVE LEFT:** A column of 7.5 Pak Marder II anti-tank guns in a Russian village. There were three marks of Marder *"Marten"*.

**BELOW:** The low silhouette of assault guns made them very effective in defence where they could be camouflaged and sited in ambush.

## STURMGESCHÜTZ III AUSF A

The reliable Panzerkampfwagen III provided the chassis for most of the Sturmgeschütz or assault guns. These low-silhouette vehicles, widely known by the abbreviation StuG, had no turret and a gun with elevation but limited traverse and were originally designed to support infantry attacks.

During the war production increased as the vehicle was less complex than a tank and kept the PzKpfw III production line running. In 1940 184 were produced, in 1941, 550 and in 1942, 828. Following the defeat at Stalingrad Germany geared up for full production and the figure jumped to 3,319; in 1944 it was 7,628 and *Sturmgeschütz* III were still being produced in 1945. The first vehicle was ordered on June 15, 1936 from Daimler-Benz and went into production in 1940 and saw limited action in France in 1940.

| | |
|---|---|
| Armament: | 7.5cm (3in) |
| Armour: | 50-30mm (2in-1.1in) |
| Crew: | 4 |
| Weight: | 19,810kg (19.5 tons) |
| Hull length: | 5.38m (17ft 6in) |
| Width: | 2.92m (9ft 5in) |
| Height: | 1.95m (6ft 3in) |
| Engine: | Maybach HL120 TRM V-12 300bhp petrol |
| Road speed: | 40km/h (25mph) |
| Range: | 100km (62.1 miles) (cross-country) |

# COUNTER ATTACK

*This is the first time in this war that I have ordered a withdrawal over a size-able section of the front. I expect the movement to be carried out in a manner worthy of the German Army. Our men's confidence in their innate superiority and their absolute determination to cause the enemy as much damage as possible must also condition the way in which this withdrawal is carried out.*

*Adolf Hitler*
*Orders issued January 15, 1942*

On December 6 the Red Army under General Zhukov launched the counter attack at Moscow. It appeared ambitious, with attacks along a wide front by the North-Western Front, Kalinin Front, Western Front and South-Western Fronts that began in December and built up into the New Year. There was even an airborne landing on January 18-22 by the 21st Parachute Brigade and 250th Airborne Regiment to the rear of the forces of German Army Group Centre facing Moscow.

*Stavka* (High Command) did not realise that the German attacks had literally frozen

in their tracks and still saw the threat to Moscow as extremely serious. Their attacks were prompted as much by desperation to take the pressure off the city than as a move to exploit their tactical advantage in winter warfare. In fact the three fronts were outnumbered by the German forces at Army Group Centre – they had 718,800 men, 7,985 guns and 720 tanks, while the Germans had 800,000 men, 14,000 guns and 1,000 tanks. The German forces were now operating at the end of a long logistic chain that stretched back through western Russia to Poland and bases in Germany. Though attacks by partisans had not become the threat that they would pose in 1942-43, and particularly in the last two years of the war, following Stalin's broadcast of July 3, 1941, they were beginning to disrupt the free flow of supplies.

The Red Air Force that had been virtually eliminated in the opening months of *Barbarossa* was becoming a real threat to the *Luftwaffe*. The obsolete slow types like the big radial-engined Polikarpovs had been destroyed in the air and on the ground, but now fighters like the Lavochkin LAGG-3, Mikoyan-Gurevitch MiG-3 and the Yakovlev

**LEFT:** Soviet paratroops board a Tupolev TB-3 (ANT-6) bomber. They exited by a hatch in the fuselage roof, sliding off the wing.

**ABOVE:** An 8.8cm Flak crew prepare to engage Soviet armour. Firing AP (armour piercing) ammunition, it had muzzle velocity of 795 metres a second.

YAK-1 operating from airfields with heated hangars located around Moscow were able to intercept German bombers.

On December 4 the chief-of-staff of the OKH *(Oberkommando des Heeres)* – German High Command – General Franz Halder noted that the German forces opposite Moscow had encountered a Soviet armoured brigade equipped with British tanks. On the same day a young *Waffen-SS* artillery officer with *Reich* wrote:

"These Russians seem to have an inexhaustible supply of men. Here they unload fresh troops from Siberia every day; they bring up fresh guns and lay mines all over the place. On the 30th we made our last attack – a hill known as Pear Hill and a village called Lenino. With artillery and mortar support we managed to take all of the hill and half of the village. But at night we had to give it all up again in order to defend ourselves more effectively against continuous Russian counter-attacks. We only needed 13 kilometres (8 miles) to get the capital within gun range – but we just could not make it."

The first Soviet attack in the early hours of December 5 was by General Ivan Konev's

Kalinin Front whose troops punched across the frozen waters of the Upper Volga. Despite the severe cold the German resistance was so strong that only one of the three armies, the 31st under Yushkevich, enjoyed any success. By the end of the second day it had penetrated nearly 40km (25 miles) and recaptured the town of Turginovo.

Lavochkin LaGG-3

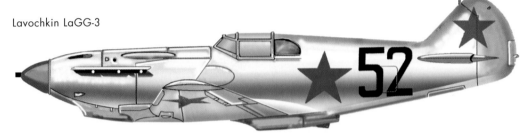

## LAVOCHKIN LaGG-3

The least successful of the LaGG series, the LaGG-3 bore the brunt of the German air attacks at the commencement of *Barbarossa* and suffered heavily at the hands of the *Luftwaffe's* Bf109s. It was replaced by the La-5 in late 1942. The Finnish Air Force operated three captured LaGG-3s. Total production was 6,528.

| | |
|---|---|
| Type: | Single-engined fighter |
| Crew: | 1 |
| Power Plant: | One 1,210hp M-105PF |
| Performance: | Maximum speed at sea level 495 km/h (308mph) |
| Maximum range: | 650km (404 miles) |
| Weights: | Empty 2,620kg (5,776lb) Maximum 3,190kg (7,032lb) |
| Dimensions: | Wing span 9.8m (32ft 1in) Length 8.82m (28ft 11in) |
| Armament: | One 20mm ShVAK cannon firing through the propeller hub; two 12.7mm UBS MG in upper cowling; provision for 200kg (440lb) of bombs or six underwing 82mm RS 82 rockets |

## MIKOYAN-GUREVITCH MiG-3

The MiG-3 was intended as a high-altitude interceptor but fared badly in 1941. It was later equipped with under-wing bombs and rockets for ground attack operations, but even in this role was not a success. It was withdrawn from front line units in the winter of 1942-43.

| | |
|---|---|
| Type: | Single-engined interceptor fighter |
| Crew: | 1 |
| Power Plant: | One 1,350hp Mikulin AM-35A |
| Performance: | Maximum speed at 7,800m (25,590ft) 640km/h (398mph) |
| Normal range: | 1,250km (777 miles) |
| Weights: | Empty 2,595kg (5,721lb) Loaded 3,350kg (7,385lb) |
| Dimensions: | Wing span 10.3m (33ft 9in) Length 8.15m (26ft 9in) Height 3.50m (11ft 6in) |
| Armament: | Two fixed forward-firing 7.62mm ShKAS MG plus one 12.7mm Beresin BS MG in upper cowling; provision for 200kg (440lb) bombs or six 82mm RS 82 rockets under wing |

Mikoyan-Gurevitch MiG-3

On December 6 Zhukov's West Front attacked the over-extended *Panzergruppen* III and IV. The attack was initially undertaken by the three most northerly armies who made slow progress even when the 16th Army joined in on December 7. The Soviet tactics of frontal assaults were being held and the Germans were withdrawing in good order. At Stalin's bidding Zhukov switched to flanking attacks focussing on the key town of Klin to the north of Moscow that straddled the railway link to Leningrad. If Zhukov could capture it quickly, *Panzergruppe* III would be cut off and the left flank of Army Group

## YAKOVLEV YAK-1

Some 400 Yak-1 fighters were available in June 1941 and 8,720 were built during the war. It was the first of a series of successful designs from the Yakovlev design bureau and was replaced by the Yak-3. The Yak-1 initially equipped the all-woman 586th Fighter Regiment and the French volunteer "*Normandy-Niémen*" fighter squadron as well as the first of four Polish volunteer units.

| | |
|---|---|
| Type: | Single-engined fighter |
| Crew: | 1 |
| Power Plant: | One 1,100hp Klimov M-105PA |
| Performance: | Maximum speed at sea level 500km/h (311mph) |
| Maximum range: | 850km (528 miles) |
| Weights: | Empty 2,330kg (5,137lb) Loaded 2,820kg (6,217lb) |
| Dimensions: | Wing span 10m (32ft 9in) Length 8.47m (27ft 9in) Height 2.64m (8ft 8in) |
| Armament: | One 20mm ShVAK cannon firing through the propeller hub; two 7.62mm ShKAS machine guns in the upper cowling; max bomb load 200kg (440lb) or six 82mm RS-82 rocket projectiles. |

**ABOVE:** *Luftwaffe* Flak crews watch an officer as he cuts a souvenir from the fuselage of a downed Soviet fighter.

# MARSHAL GEORGI ZHUKOV (1896-1974)

Zhukov, who would become one of the finest leaders of the Soviet Army, had modest beginnings. Born of peasant stock near Moscow, like many of Stalin's cronies, he had been a Cavalry NCO in the Imperial Russian Army that he entered at the age of 15. He joined the Communist Party in 1919. Unlike other generals from this background like Voroshilov and Budenny, he was tough and highly competent. His nicknames with the frontoviks – front line soldiers – were "Vinegar Face" or "Cropped-Head".

In September 1939 the then little known General Zhukov inflicted a sharp defeat on the Japanese Kwantung Army on the Halha River at Khalkin-Gol in Outer Mongolia. His skilful handling of five armoured brigades expelled the Japanese 6th or Kanto Army from its positions that it had captured on the Mongolian Manchurian border. The Japanese commander, who had disobeyed orders and invaded Soviet territory, had air superiority and had assembled three infantry divisions, 180 tanks, 500 guns and 450 aircraft. The Russians had 100,000 infantry with 498 tanks, strong artillery and 580 outclassed aircraft. Zhukov used his infantry to hold the Japanese front and then launched his armour in a pincer attack. The Soviet losses were about 10,000 but the shaken Japanese withdrew after suffering losses of about 18,000.

For this Zhukov received the Order of Lenin. At Leningrad he was seen as halting the German attack and so Stalin moved him to Moscow. Here poor weather, fatigue and stiffening Russian resistance halted the attack and, using reinforcements from the Far East, Zhukov attacked in December and remained on the offensive until March 1942.

At Stalingrad he would master-mind Operation Uranus, the counter attack, that was followed by Operation Saturn that forced Germans back to the River Donets. In January 1943 he was promoted to the rank of Marshal.

At Kursk Soviet forces under his overall command halted the German attacks and then rolled onto an unstoppable offensive. In Operation Bagration in June and July 1944 he destroyed Army Group Centre, finally leading the First Belorussian Front to victory in Berlin in 1945.

Resentful of his popularity, Stalin banished him to command a remote military district after the war. Zhukov would, however, rise to be Minister of Defence in the USSR in 1953 following Stalin's death.

**ABOVE:** A German sentry on a bridge. He is wearing woven reed overboots as protection against the cold. Leather soled boots with metal studs were poor protection in the winter.

## PISTOLET-PULEMET SHPAGINA o1941g

Soviet troops were principally armed with the robust and very effective *Pistolet-Pulemet Shpagina o1941g* or PPSh-41 submachine gun. This weapon used simple production techniques of stamping and brazing, weighed 3.56kg (7.8lb) and had a 71-round drum or 35-round box magazine. It fired at 900 rounds a minute, a rate of fire that in Korea would earn it the nickname, the "Burp Gun". The gun designed by G.S. Shpagin used barrels taken from bolt-action Mosin Nagant M1891/30 rifles that were chromed to reduce corrosion and wear. The drum magazine held 71 rounds of 7.62mm pistol ammunition and the box 35. By 1945 some 5,000,000 had been produced. In Leningrad, where there were munitions factories, but wood was almost unobtainable, A.I. Sudarev designed the Pistolet-Pulemet Sudareva o1943g or PPS43 sub-machine gun, an all-metal weapon with a folding stock and a 35-round box magazine. This modern design was produced after the war.

Centre unhinged. The staff of the West and Bryansk Fronts were not as experienced in planning and operational skills and the ambitious flanking attacks would prove difficult to control and co-ordinate.

On December 7, as Field Marshal von Leeb was receiving reports from the front lines and adjusting the deployment of his forces to meet these threats, he was informed that new attacks were being launched, directed against his right flank. In Berlin Field Marshal Walther von Brauchitsch, the Commander in Chief of the German Army (OKH), who had recently suffered a heart attack, tendered his resignation to Hitler, who did not accept it.

On December 13 Timoshenko's South West Front began to attack north-westwards between Yelets and Livny. His 13th Army ripped into the left flank of the German 2nd Army, forcing Guderian to make a hurried withdrawal as his right flank was exposed and vulnerable.

Von Brauchitsch flew to Russia to confer with Bock and decided that Army Group Centre should withdraw to a "Winter Line" about 180km (111 miles) west of the front line. The line followed the north-south roadway just east of Vyazma through Zubtsov, Gzhatsk and Yukhnov. In the OKH General Halder pronounced the Soviet counter attack as "the greatest crisis in two World Wars" – there would be greater to come.

**BELOW :** Soldiers attempt to warm up around a fire. The cold sapped morale and caused many crippling injuries.

**ABOVE:** A 21cm *Mörser* 18 with whitewash camouflage. The crews could fire one shell every two minutes.

**BELOW:** Signallers with a Torn.Fu d2 two-man pack radio. German radio equipment was easy to service.

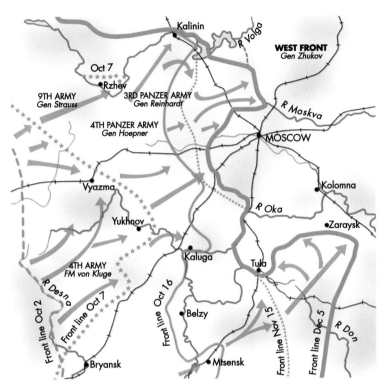

Oct 7

9TH ARMY
Gen Strauss

3RD PANZER ARMY
Gen Reinhardt

4TH PANZER ARMY
Gen Hoepner

WEST FRONT
Gen Zhukov

R Volga

Kalinin

Rzhev

R Moskva

MOSCOW

Vyazma

Yukhnov

Kolomna

R Oka

Zaraysk

4TH ARMY
FM von Kluge

Kaluga

Tula

R Desna

Front line Oct 2

Front line Oct 7

Front line Oct 16

Belzy

Front line Nov 15

Front line Dec 5

R Don

Bryansk

Mtsensk

**LEFT:** The final attack on Moscow. To Hitler the city seemed within his grasp, but the Panzer divisions were now under strength in men and vehicles and all the soldiers were exhausted. Soviet troops were fighting with a new determination and finally "General Winter" had come to their assistance.

**BELOW:** Ski-mounted soldiers practise taking cover. For cross-country operations German soldiers had lightweight skis with special bindings that made the skis interchangeable.

In Berlin Hitler was enraged by the withdrawal and on December 14 countermanded the orders and initiated a round of sackings. The gaunt von Bock, now a sick man, was replaced by von Kluge on December 18 and on Christmas Day Guderian, the Panzer expert, was sacked, along with another exponent of armoured warfare, General Erich Höpner. On December 19 Hitler, the former World War I corporal, accepted the resignation of von Brauchitsch and assumed command of the German Army.

**BELOW:** The Henschel Hs123A-1 was a tough and very effective close-support aircraft liked by its crews and soldiers on the ground.

# HENSCHEL Hs123A-1

The rugged fixed-undercarriage biplane looked like an aircraft from World War I, but would serve from 1936 to 1944. After about 60 had been built, production was halted in 1938, but there were demands from front-line formations that it should be recommenced. Though the Hs123A-1 might be obsolescent it was still a very effective ground-attack aircraft.

| Type: | Single-engined ground attack fighter/dive bomber |
|---|---|
| Crew: | 1 |
| Power Plant: | One 870hp BMW 132D 9-cylinder radial |
| Performance: | Maximum speed at 12,200m (3,940ft) 342km/h (213 mph) |
| Maximum range: | 860km (534 miles) |
| Weights: | Empty 1,504kg (3,316lb) Normal 2,217kg (4,888lb) |
| Dimensions: | Wing span upper 10.50m (34ft 5in) Wing span lower 8m (26ft 3in) Length 8.33m (27ft 4in) |
| Armament: | Two 7.92mm MG 17 machine guns; max bomb load 450kg (992lb) |

**Above:** A corpse lies in the snow by a knocked out KV1 heavy tank. It appears to have hit an anti-tank mine. Its running gear is smashed and a track is missing.

From December 15, on the day that Klin was liberated, the threat to Moscow diminished and the government ministers begun to return to their posts from the towns to the east where they had been evacuated.

On December 18 the Bryansk Front under General Cherevichenko was established to the south of Moscow. It would attack northwestwards to assist in a double envelopment of Army Group Centre.

On December 19, 1941 Hitler issued a General Order:

"Commanders and officers must, by way of personal participation in the fighting, compel

**Right:** An MG34 gunner peers cautiously around the corner during a standing patrol of outlying buildings near the German front line.

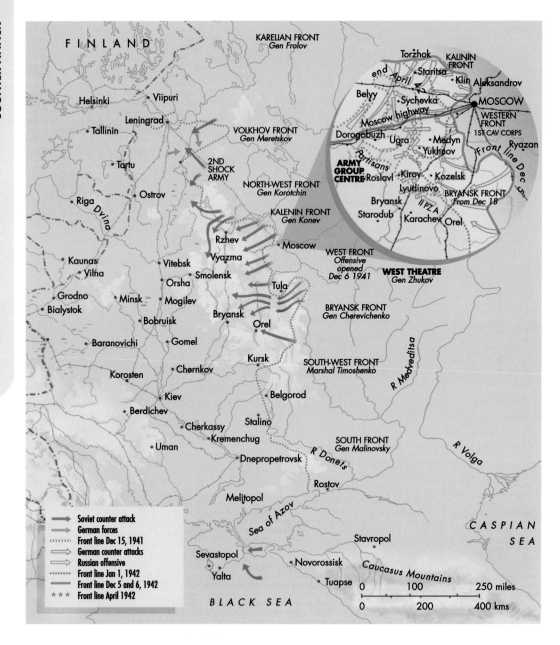

**ABOVE:** The Soviet counter attack was not just confined to taking the pressure off Moscow. It was also intended to relieve the sieges of Leningrad and Sevastopol. The operations around Moscow were the most ambitious, with parachute drops and attacks by Partisans. With reports of German soldiers withdrawing, Hitler ordered that they should stand and fight. Though this prevented a complete collapse, he began to see it as the panacea for all Soviet offensives.

## ZOIA KOSMODEMIANSKAIA

Among the photographs found near Moscow following the Soviet counter offensive were snapshots of the last moments of a young Russian girl named Zoia Kosmodemianskaia who was hanged by the Germans on November 29, 1941. The Germans had hung a sign around her neck saying "She set fire to houses" – a common practice intended to explain why the sentence had been carried out and to deter other would-be partisans. Kosmodemianskaia was caught while she attempted to set fire to stables housing German Army horses in the village of Petrischevo. Just before her execution the *Komsomol* (Young Communist) member turned to her executioners and said: "You can't hang all 190 million of us".

Two weeks later in the Soviet counter offensive a Pravda war reporter named Lidin found the photographs and photographed her body in the snow with the noose still in place. His account of her death turned her into a symbol of resistance and a Partisan heroine.

the troops to offer fanatical resistance in their positions, regardless of enemy breakthroughs on the flank and rear. Only after well-prepared shortened rearward positions have been manned by reserves may withdrawal to such positions be considered."

Where troops were forced back Hitler insisted that they destroy the buildings that could be used as shelter by the advancing Soviet forces. Though this scorched earth policy was followed in some withdrawals, many Germans knew that smoke would attract roving Soviet patrols and it was self interest that prompted them to spare some of the thatched wooden or mud brick houses.

General Schaal, commanding the 10th Panzer Division, paints a grim picture of the withdrawal: "Discipline began to crack. There were more and more soldiers making their own way back to the west, without any weapons, leading a calf on a rope, or drawing a sledge with potatoes behind them – just trudging westward with no one in command.

**BELOW:** Stripped of his boots a Russian soldier with a DP light machine gun frozen in the last attitudes of death.

Men killed by aerial bombardment were no longer buried. Supply units, frequently without officers, had the decisive way on the roads, while the fighting troops of all branches, including anti-aircraft artillery, were desperately holding out in the front line. The entire supply train – except where units were firmly led – was streaming back in wild flight." It was the first German retreat of World War II.

# KLIMENTI VOROSHILOV 1

Taking the cumbersome dual turreted T-100, Z. Kotin, the chief engineer of the Kirov-Zavod factory, designed a more compact tank that was originally known as the Kotin-Stalin but designated Klimenti-Voroshilov (KV). The KV-1 was upgraded during its operational life, the most important changes being the KV-1A longer L/41.5 76.2mm gun and the KV-1B and C that had cast turrets. It was unstable and very vulnerable. In June 1941 the Soviet Army had 508 KV-1s in the field. The KV-2 (Above) used the same chassis but was armed with a huge 152mm howitzer. It was intended for a direct support role. One KV-2 astonished the Germans of Army Group Centre when it survived 11 hits from PzKpfw III 7.5cm guns.

| | |
|---|---|
| Armament: | 76.2mm (3in), 4 x 7.62mm MG |
| Armour: | 100mm (3.94in) |
| Crew: | 5 |
| Weight: | 42,910kg (42.23 tons) |
| Hull length: | 6.68m (21ft 11in) |
| Width: | 3.32m (10ft 10in) |
| Height: | 2.71m (8ft 10in) |
| Engine: | V-2K V-12 diesel engine developing 600hp Road |
| speed: | 35km/h (21.75mph |
| Range: | 150km (93.2 miles) |

**RIGHT:** Soviet soldiers in the Leningrad garrison manhandle a 45mm (1.77in) Model 1932 anti-tank gun. Firing a 1.43kg shell, the little gun could penetrate 38mm (1.4in) of armour at 0.9km (1,000yd).

In the south in bitter weather on December 29 Soviet soldiers and naval infantry made a landing at Feodosiya in the Crimea and pushed back the German forces in the east of the peninsula. Just over two weeks later the South West Front under Marshal Timoshenko attacked Army Group South. Stalin had grand ambitions, hoping that they would be able to trap the Germans against the Sea of Azov in a huge pocket. The Soviet forces reached the River Orel and cut the Kharkov to Lozovaya railway but the attack finally halted in the spring mud in early March.

To the north on January 7 Stalin ordered General Kirill Merestkov, commanding the newly created Volkhov Front, to attack and destroy the German forces to the north of Lake Ilmen on the line of the River Volkhov.

On a narrow front he committed the 59th Army, 2nd Shock Army and 52nd Army. The weather that had been an enemy for the Germans now came to their aid and the attack foundered in mud in the March thaw. Despite this Stalin insisted that the Soviet forces should not withdraw and the 62km (38.5-mile) salient was pinched out in June by German counter attacks. Among the prisoners captured was the commanding officer of the 2nd Shock Army Lt General Andrey Vlasov. Vlasov had distinguished himself earlier in the defence of Moscow and realised that Stalin's orders had condemned him and his men to death or capture. A loyal Soviet general he now became a disenchanted ally of the Germans.

In the offensive the town of Demyansk south of Lake Ilmen was cut off by the 3rd

## OSTMEDAILLE

German soldiers who survived the winter of 1941-42 in Russia received the *Medaille Winterschlacht im Osten*, 1941/42. The medal, instituted by Hitler on May 26, 1942, was designed by *SS-Unterscharführer* Ernst Kraus. It consisted of a black disc surmounted with a silver helmet and grenade at the top. On the obverse there was the *Reichsadler* while the reverse had a bayonet and laurel frond with the words "*Winterschlacht in Osten 1941/42*". It had a distinctive pink ribbon with a fine black stripe in the centre flanked by a white stripe. This ribbon was normally worn buttoned through the front of the soldier's tunic.

Criteria for its award were: 1) Minimum of two weeks of combat; 2) *Luftwaffe* personnel, 30 days over enemy territory; 3) Wounds or frozen limbs for which the Wound Badge was awarded; 4) Minimum of 60 days in the combat zone. The "East" was designated as the area east of the Ukraine and Ostland.

The Winter Campaign medal was also known as the *Ostmedaille* – Eastern Medal – or, in the *Landsers'* grim slang, the *Gefrierfleischorden*, the Cold Meat Medal or, more kindly, the Frost Medal.

**LEFT:** Well equipped *Waffen-SS* troops with their SdKfz 251 half track in a local counter attack against a defended village.

Shock Army and 34th Army, part of the North-West Front under General Korotchin. Some 100,000 men of the Army Group North, 2nd Army Corps and *Waffen-SS* 3rd SS-Panzer-Division "*Totenkopf*" were trapped in the pocket for a 14-month siege from February 8, to April 21, 1942. The troops were re-supplied by air and though they suffered 3,335 killed and 10,966 wounded they were eventually able to break out on April 21, 1942. The defence of the pocket had tied down 18 Soviet divisions and six brigades that could have assisted in the winter offensive of 1941-42. Field Marshal von Leeb, commanding Army Group North, who had requested permission to withdraw, volun-tarily relinquished his command.

**LEFT:** As the Sd Kfz 251 prepares to move off, men climb over the side that is screened from enemy fire.

**ABOVE:** Smoke swirls around the vehicle as it prepares to withdraw. Shelters and personal kit are strapped to the mudguards.

**ABOVE:** Field Marshal Fedor von Bock in happier times confers over a map table in his camouflaged field HQ in the summer of 1941.

**RIGHT:** Field Marshal Walther von Brauchitsch, Army Commander in Chief, who was sacked by Hitler on December 19, 1941. He was a cautious and unpolitical officer who, despite the Blitzkrieg triumphs of the first three years of the war, was not widely respected.

**ABOVE:** A German 5cm *Leichter Granatenwerfer* 36 crew in the first snows of 1941.

The successful defence of these small pockets and the "stand and fight" order that actually prevented the collapse of Army Group Centre would be seen by Hitler as a panacea for all subsequent battles of encirclement. A year later, with fateful consequences, he would issue similar orders to the 6th Army at Stalingrad.

In the south, where Hitler had sacked von Rundstedt, commanding Army Group South, following withdrawals in the Crimea, his replacement, Von Reichenau, died of a heart attack on January 18 and was in turn replaced by von Bock.

The fighting had lasted from December 1941 to March 1942 and in that time, in some sectors around Moscow, German forces had been pushed back as much as 500km (310 miles).

In the five months from June 22 to November 26, 1941 187,000 men were killed or posted missing in the German armed forces. The wounded for this period were 555,000, of whom two thirds might be expected to return to duty. The killed and missing for the whole of the Eastern Front from November 27 to March 31, 1942 were put at 108,000 and the wounded at 268,000, a total of 376,000 men. To this figure must be added 228,000 frost-bite cases and over a quarter of a million other sick, mainly from exhaustion, exposure, typhus, scarlet fever, jaundice, diphtheria and stomach and skin complaints. Most of these were the result of the terrible conditions in which front line troops were expected to live. By April the overall deficiency in manpower in the East stood at 625,000.

Men were not the only casualties of the fighting. A quarter of a million horses, half of those that had entered Russia, perished in the bitter cold. The Germans lost 2,300 armoured vehicles, of which 1,600 were either PzKpfw

**ABOVE**: A German Horch 4 x 4 108 heavy car stuck in the deep Russian snow.

**BELOW**: Greatcoat-clad MG34 machine gun sections on the move.

**RIGHT:** The Soviet KV1 heavy tank: tough armour and a 76.2mm gun.

**ABOVE:** A 10.5cm leFH 18 crew prepare ammunition. In extreme cold lubricants became viscous and grease hard – small fires were needed to thaw weapons.

Mk III or Mk IV tanks or assault guns. In April the artillery were short of 2,000 guns and howitzers and 7,000 anti-tank guns.

Now, just as Stalin was listening to the advice of his senior commanders, Hitler was dismissing suggestions that German forces should withdraw to avoid being cut off in vulnerable salients. Hitler's tactics were described by Halder as *Flickwerk* – patchwork. Defences were cobbled together to restore breaks by deploying troops from other areas. Stalin, however, was giving his

**RIGHT:** In a white smock a German infantryman looks well prepared for the winter. In reality few had suitable clothing or camouflage.

**ABOVE:** German soldiers move cautiously through woodland. Artillery airbursts could be lethal and scrub and snow offered cover for Soviet snipers.

commanders strategic objectives, what today would be called "mission statements". They were tasked with defence or attack, but given freedom to conduct operations in the manner they thought was most effective at a tactical level. It was a winning formula.

With the onset of the spring mud the front finally stabilised. Territory had been liberated in the north, producing a large salient with a series of smaller salients, like the truncated

## A SYMPHONY FOR A CITY

In March 1942 the town of Kuibyshev on the Volga hosted the first performance of Symphony No 7 Op 60 in C Major by the 34-year-old composer Dimitri Shostakovich (1906-1975). It was "Dedicated to the City of Leningrad" and the initial work had been done by Shostakovich while he was a volunteer fireman in the city, before, in October 1941, Stalin ordered that he be flown out to Kuibyshev. It is a powerful work that Shostakovich described as:"inspired by the great events of our Patriotic War, but it is not battle music.

The first movement is dedicated to the struggle, and the last movement to victory. No more noble mission can be conceived than our fight against the dark powers of Hitlerism. The roar of cannons will not keep the muses of our people from lifting their strong voices".

The score was microfilmed, flown out of the USSR and first performed in the United States, conducted by Toscanini with the NBC Symphony Orchestra, in July 1942.

## LT GENERAL ANDREY VLASOV (1900–1946)

Born at Lomkino near Nizhni Novgorod on September 1, 1900, Vlasov joined the Red Army in 1919. When Germany invaded Russia he had risen to the rank of general and commanded the 4th Tank Corps. He defended Kiev in September 1941 as C-in-C 37th Army. He played a successful part in the

defence of Moscow in December 1941. In March 1942, commanding the 2nd Shock Army on the Volkhov Front, his forces were surrounded and he was captured on July 11. Disenchanted with Stalin's leadership, he put himself at the disposal of the *Smolensker Komitee*, a group of anti-Stalin Russian soldiers and politicians and wrote leaflets that were dropped behind Russian lines urging Russian soldiers to desert. He sought to set up a military formation to fight the Soviet forces. The Germans used him for propaganda, but only at the end of the war was he given command of the Vlasov Army, a force of two divisions dressed in German uniforms with distinctive arm shield insignia. Their weapons were largely captured ones of Soviet origin. Captured by the British at the end of the war he was handed over to the Soviet Union, tried for treason in Moscow and executed on August 2, 1946.

fingers of a huge hand, facing south-west towards Vitebsk. To the south a German salient had been created with Vyazma at its base and Rzhev at its northernmost point. Hitler would delude himself that this was a potential jumping off point for a renewed attack on Moscow in the summer of 1942. Vyazma was held until the spring of 1943 and during its occupation thousands of young men and women were deported to Nazi Germany as slave labourers. Prior to their withdrawal the Germans destroyed practically the whole city.

To the south the long salient that had

**LEFT:** Snow covers the bodies of Soviet soldiers caught frozen in tortured attitudes of death following a failed attack.

hooked around Tula had been eliminated by the Bryansk Front and the front line effectively straightened out into a rough north-south line. Zhukov's West Front had pushed towards the Dniepr north of Bryansk to produced a small salient.

The counter offensive liberated areas that had been under German control and revealed the brutal character of *Rassenkampf* and the German occupation. It provided further fuel to the fire of anger felt by many Russians.

In Moscow the Russian Ilya Ehrenburg, writing in the Soviet Army newspaper *Red Star*, commented dryly on the successful counter attack and the German Army's experience of the winter of 1941-1942.

"The Russian winter was a surprise for the Prussian tourists".

COUNTER ATTACK

**ABOVE**: The German cemetery constructed at Yasnaya Polyana, near the home and grave of the Russian writer Tolstoy, south of Moscow. This would be the limit of the 1941 advance into the USSR.

# INDEX

AA gun, 37mm, 42
Abbeville, 33
Africa, North, 44
*Afrika Korps*, 25
Air Regiment 588th, 54
Albania, 26
Anti Tank Gun, 57mm, 58
Archangel, 31
Army 2nd, 75
Army 2nd (Soviet), 53
Army 2nd Shock (Soviet), 83, 93
Army 3rd (Rumanian), 15
Army 3rd (Soviet), 19
Army 3rd Shock (Soviet), 85
Army 4th, 15, 51
Army 4th (Rumanian), 15
Army 5th (Soviet), 19
Army 6th, 15, 87
Army 6th (Soviet), 19, 42
Army 6th, Kanto, (Japanese), 74
Army 7th (Soviet), 19
Army 8th (Soviet), 19
Army 9th, 15, 51
Army 9th (Soviet), 19
Army 10th (Soviet), 19
Army 11th, 15, 44
Army 11th (Soviet), 19
Army 12th (Soviet), 19, 42
Army 13th (Soviet), 75
Army 14th (Soviet), 19
Army 16th, 15
Army 16th (Soviet), 73
Army 17th, 15
Army 18th, 15, 30
Army 18th (Soviet), 19, 42
Army 20th (Soviet), 62
Army 23rd (Soviet), 19
Army 31st (Soviet), 72
Army 33rd (Soviet), 62
Army 52nd (Soviet), 83
Army 59th (Soviet), 83
Army Corps 2nd, 85
Army Group Centre, 11, 15, 20, 24, 34, 36, 62, 71, 74, 75, 79, 87
Army Group North, 11, 15, 20, 24, 26, 40, 41, 42, 49, 85
Army Group South, 11, 15, 20, 24, 33, 49, 83, 87
Army, Independent Maritime, 44
Army, Kwantung, 63, 74
Arnim, Jurgen von, 51
Astrakhan, 31
Atlantic Wall, 16
Axis, 33
Azov, Sea of, 83

BA-10, 47
Babi Yar, 11
Badaev food warehouse, 40
Bagration, Operation, 74
Baltic, 23, 40
Balkans, 33, 44
*Barbarossa*, 4, 6, 12, 14, 22, 25, 60, 63, 71, 72
Belgium, 10, 57
Belgrade, 33
Belorussia, 7
Beria, Lavrenti, 8
Berlin, 20, 52, 74, 75
Bershanskaya, Yevdokiya, 55
Bessarabia, 20
Bf109F, Messerschmitt, 25, 72
Black Forest, 62
Black Sea, 44
*Blitzkrieg*, 5, 23, 36, 38
BMW R75, 51, 68
Bock, Fedor von, 15, 20, 24, 33, 75, 78, 86, 87
Borisov, Raskova 125th Regiment, 54
Brandenburgers, 24
Brauchitsch, Walther von, 75, 78, 86
Brest-Litovsk, 11, 20, 22, 24
Brigade 21st (Soviet Parachute), 70
Brno, 57
Bryansk, 51, 52
BT-2
BT-7, 21, 42
Budenny, Semyon, 31, 34, 51
Bug, River, 7, 20, 24
Bukovina, 20
Busch, Ernst von, 15
Byalistok, 24, 27, 28

Caucasus, 33
Caudillo, 39
Celere, Division, 44
Chelyabinsk, 54
Cherevichenko, Ya T., 19, 79
China, 8
Christie, Walter, 21
Churchill, Winston, 7, 28
Ciuperca, 15
Cossacks, 33
Crimea, 83, 87
Cripps, Stafford, 7
Croats, 25
CSIR, 42
Czechoslovakia, 57

Daugavpils, 26
Degtyarev, Alexeyevich, 37
Decker, 59

Demyansk, 83
Desna, 51
Dive Bomber Regiment 587th, 54
Division, 29th, 61
Division, 45th, 24, 68
Division, 250th, 39
*Division Azul*, 39
Dniepr, 16, 93
Dniestr, 16
Dog Mines, 53
Don, 36, 61
DP LMG, 37, 81
Dubno, 24
Duce, 44
Dumitrescu, 15
Dunkirk, 46
Dvina, 26

Ehrenburg, Ilya, 93
*Einsatzcommandos*, 11
*Einsatzgruppen*, 11
Eremenko, Andrey, 50
Estonia, 10, 16, 33, 40

Fedyuninsky, 24
Feodosiya, 83
Fiat 628BL, 59
Fieseler Fi56, 22
Fighter Regiment 586th, 54
Finland, 18, 20, 24, 26, 46
Finnish Air Force, 72
Finnish Army, 38, 49
FN, 57
France, 33, 44, 62
Franco, Francisco, 39
*Fritz, Fall*, 14
Frolov, V.A., 19
Front, Belorussian, 74
Front, Bryansk, 50, 75, 79, 93
Front, Kalinin, 70, 72
Front, North Western, 70, 85
Front, Reserve, 50
Front, South Western, 70, 75, 83
Front, Volkov, 83, 93
Front, West, 50, 52, 62, 70, 73, 75, 93

Germany, 57
Goebbels, Josef, 63
Golubev, K.D., 19
Gorelenko, G.A., 19
Gorki, 31, 56
GRU, 8
Guderian, Heinz, 15, 33, 50, 51, 62, 66, 75, 78
*Gulag*, 23
Gzhatsk, 75

Halder, Franz, 31, 71, 75, 90
Hamburg, 20
Harnack, Arvid, 10

Harnack, Mildred, 10
Henschel Hs123, 78
Hitler, Adolf, 9, 11, 30, 44, 70, 75, 78, 79, 81, 86, 87, 90
Höpner, Erich, 15, 59, 62, 78
Hoth, Herman, 15
Hungary, 18, 20, 26

Ilmen, Lake, 42, 83
Infantes, Esteban, 39

Japan, 63, 68, 74
Jews, 9
Junkers Ju52, 44, 65

Kar 98k, 57
Karelian Peninsula, 26
Karl, 60cm mortar, 24, 27
Kashira, 59
Katukov, 62
*Katyusha* M-8, 32, 34
Keller, Alfred, 20
Kesselring, Albert, 20, 23, 40
Khabarovsk, 68
Khalkin-Gol, 74
Kharkov, 31, 83
Kiev, 11, 23, 30, 31, 33, 34, 49, 93
Kirov, 56
Kirponos, M.P., 19
Kleist, Ewald von, 15, 33
Klin, 73, 79
Kluge, Gunther, 15, 51, 78
Knaak, Wolfram, 26
Kolkhozes, 28
Kommissar Erlass, 11
Komsomol, 81
Konev, Ivan, 50, 71
Korobkov, A.A., 19
Korotchin, 85
Korpic, 12, 18
Koshkin, M.I., 23
Kosmodemianskaia, Zoia, 81
Kostenko, F. Ya, 19
Kovel, 24
Kovno, 26
Krasny Bor, 39
Krasnaya Polyana, 62
Kraus, Ernst, 84
Kremlin, 53
Kruschev, Nikita, 12
Kucherenko, N.A., 23
Küchler, George von, 15
Kuibyshev, 53, 92
Kursk, 74
Kuznetsov, F.I., 19
KV-1, 79, 82, 88
KV-2, 82

Ladoga, Lake, 18, 49

Latvia, 10, 16, 27, 33
Lavochkin LAGG-3, 71, 72
Leeb, Ritter von, 15, 20, 49, 75, 85
LeFH, 10.5cm, 90
Leningrad, 18, 26, 31, 36, 37, 39, 40, 41, 46, 74, 92
Lenino, 71
Lidin, 81
Lines of Communications Divisions, 20
Lithuania, 10, 16, 24, 33
Litvak, Lilya, 54
Livny, 75
Löhr, Alexander, 20
Lotta, 38
Lozovaya, 83
*Luftwaffe*, 23, 25, 36, 44, 46, 54, 55, 71
*Luftflotte* I, 20
*Luftflotte* II, 20, 40
*Luftflotte* IV, 20
*Luftflotte* V, 20

M3 Half Track, 20
Maginot Line, 27
Manchuria, 63, 68, 74
Mannerheim, Gustav, 49
Marcks, 30
*Marder* II, 69
Markov, Valentin, 55
Maxim MG, 42, 49
Mendeleeva, Berte, 54
Merestkov, Kirill, 83
Messe, Giovanni, 44
MG34, 53, 54, 63, 79, 88
Mikhaylov, 61
Mikoyan-Gurevitch MiG-3, 71, 72
Minsk, 33
Molotov Cocktail, 52
Mongolia, 74
Morosov, A.A., 23
Morosov, V.I., 19
Mörser 18, 76
Moscow, 5, 23, 25, 30, 40, 41, 49, 52, 53, 56, 59, 61, 63, 65, 67, 70, 73, 74, 77, 79, 80, 81, 87, 93, 95
Mosin Nagant, 75
Mozhaisk, 52, 56
Munoz Grandes, Augustin, 39
Murmansk, 18, 20
Mussolini, Benito, 44
Muzychenko, I.N., 19

Napoleon I, 22
Nizhni Novgorod, 93
NKVD, 8, 34, 52
Norway, 44
Novgorod, 42
Odessa, 44, 46

OKH, 71, 75
OKW, 31, 36,
Orel, 56, 83
Orsha, 34
*Ostmedaille*, 84
*Otto-Programme*, 12
Ozeretskoye, 59

Pak 3.7cm, 29
Pak 4.7cm, 21
*Panzerarmee* II, 27, 34, 50, 51, 56, 61
*Panzerarmee* III, 27, 34
*Panzerarmee* IV, 49
*Panzergruppe* I, 15, 33, 34
*Panzergruppe* II, 15, 33, 34
*Panzergruppe* III, 15, 50, 73
*Panzergruppe* IV, 15, 50, 59, 62, 73
Panzer Division, 1st, 53
Panzer Division 2nd, 59
Panzer Division 3rd, 53
Panzer Division, 3rd *Waffen-SS*, 85
Panzer Division 7th, 53, 62
Panzer Division 10th, 62, 81
Panzer Division, 17th, 52
Pasubio, Division, 44
Pavlov, D.G., 19
Pe-2, 54
Pear Hill, 71
Petrischevo, 81
Petrov, I.Y., 44
Po-2, 54
Poland, 8, 44, 49, 53, 71
Polikarpov, 71
Polikarpov I-15, 37
Ponedelin, P.D., 19
Popov, M.M., 19
Potapov, M.I., 19
PoW, 10, 12, 16, 43, 61
PPSh-41, 75
Pravda, 81
Pripet Marshes, 16
*Propagandakompanie* (PK), 6, 26
Pshennikov, P.S., 19
PzKpfw I, 21
PzKpfw III, 14, 21, 28, 31, 38, 58, 69, 82, 90
PzKpfw IV, 56, 63, 90
PzKpfw 35(t), 37

Raskova, Marina, 54
*Rasputitsa*, 5, 50
*Rassenkampf*, 11, 93
Rastenburg, 36
Red Air Force, 23, 71
Red Orchestra, 10
Red Square, 53
Regiment 69th, 62
Regiment 135th, 68
Regiment 250th (Soviet

Airborne), 70
Regiment 262nd, 39
Regiment 263rd, 39
Regiment 269th, 39
Regiment 805th (Soviet Ground Attack), 55
*Reich*, 71
Reichenau, Walter von, 15, 87
Riga, 27
Rommel, Erwin, 62
Royal Navy, 46
Ruhr, 20
Rumania, 18, 20, 23
Rumanian Army, 44
Rundstedt, Gerd von, 15, 20, 24, 26
Russia, 71
Russian Revolution, 41
*Russlandlied*, 6

Samsonov, 63
*Saturn*, Operation, 74
Schaal, 66, 81
Schobert, Eugene, 15
Scorched Earth, 18
Schulze-Boyson, Harro, 10
SdKfz 250, 31
SdKfz 251, 20, 22, 34, 85
Sevastopol, 46
Shlisselburg, 49
Shostakovich, Dimitri, 92
Shpagin, G.S., 75
Shturmovik, Illyushin, 55
Siberia, 23
*Signal*, 14, 61
Smirnov, A.K., 19
Smolensk, 34
Smolensk Pocket, 42
Sobennikov, P.P., 19
Sorge, Richard, 8, 12, 63
Spain, 39
Spitfire, Supermarine, 25
Stalin, Joseph, 7, 10, 12, 16, 20, 26, 27, 51, 53, 63, 74, 83, 90, 92
Stalin Line, 27
Stalin's Organ, 32
Stalingrad, 49, 74, 87
STAVKA, 63, 70
Strauss, Adolf, 15, 51
Stülpnagel, Karl, 15
Stumpff, Hans-Jurgen, 20
*Sturmgeschütz* III, 69
Sudarev, A.I., 75

T-26S, 29, 41
T-34/76, 23, 28, 32, 34, 54, 56
*Taifun*, Operation, 50
Tallinin, 40
Taman Guards Bomber Regiment 46th, 54, 55

Tankograd, 54
Third Reich, 64
Tilsit, 24
Timofeya-Yegorova, Anna, 55
Timoshenko, Semion, 19, 83
Tokarev SVT40, 49
Tokyo, 8
Tolstoy, Leo, 62, 95
*Torino*, Division, 44
Toscanini, 92
*Totenkopf*, 85
Trepper, Leopold, 10
Tukhachevskiy, Mikhail, 23, 68
Tula, 61, 93
Tula Arsenal, 37
Turginovo, 72
Tyuleney, IV, 19

Ugra, 59
Ukraine, 36, 46, 65
ULTRA, 8, 16
Uman Pocket, 42
Ural Mountains, 54
*Uranus*, Operation, 74
USA, 28
USSR, 10, 12, 27, 33

Velikaya, 16
Vishnyaki, 53
Vitebsk, 93
Vlasov, Andrey, 83, 93
Vlasov Army, 93
Volga, 31, 53, 72, 92
Volga Canal, 62
Volkhov, 83
Voroshilov, Klimenti, 82
Vyazma, 51, 56, 75, 93

*Waffen-SS*, 47, 51, 71, 85
Winter uniforms, 66, 67
West Wall, 16
Winter war, 18, 26
*Wolfsschanze*, 36
World War I, 8
Wound Badge, 84

Yakhroma, 62
Yakovlev, Yak-1, 54, 71, 73
Yasnaya Polyana, 62, 95
Yelets, 75
Yugoslavia, 8
Yushkevich, 72

Zhukov, Georgi, 52, 70, 73, 74, 93
Zubstov, 75